MW01280362

BASIC COURSE IN PITMAN SHORTHAND

BASIC COURSE
IN
PITMAN SHORTHAND

NEW YORK
PITMAN PUBLISHING CORPORATION

PREFACE

One of the most important contributions to the improvement of instruction in shorthand has been the compilation of a list of 700 words, chosen not only because they are so often used but also because they are suitable examples for learning the principles of the Pitman system. These 700 words, with their simple derivatives, comprise approximately 80% of all the words used in current English speech and writing. Where this list has been introduced as an approach to the subject, students have progressed faster, and notably better results have been achieved.

In the 50 lessons that follow, this list of 700 words is used as the basis for a presentation of the principles in a new form and in a new order. The presentation should accelerate still further the rate of learning and the development of a satisfactory skill; at the same time, it should make the work of both the teacher and the student more interesting and more enjoyable.

CONTENTS

TO THE STUDENT

Some of the words on this page appear in their shorthand form instead of in the familiar printed letters. You will be able, without previous instruction in shorthand, ⟍ read these words. If for each sign you will supply the word that is needed ⟍ complete the sense, you will discover the word that is represented by the shorthand sign.

You will have discovered already, for example, that the word " to " is expressed in shorthand by a small, slanting dash. (The dotted line on which the sign rests represents the ruled line of your notebook.) This small dash is written very lightly in a downward direction so that it rests on the ruled line of your paper.

⟍ next sign is a light dot which also is written on ⟍ ruled line. You will readily see that this dot expresses ⟍ word " the."

In this paragraph two additional signs are introduced. One ⟍ them is another small slanting dash. It is written lightly in a downward direction, but this time it is written above ⟍ line instead ⟍ on it. This sign, ⟍ course, represents " of." ⟍ dashes ⟍ and ⟍ have ⟍ same slope, direction, and length; ⟍ only distinction is in their position. ⟍ other sign is ⟍ light dot that is written above ⟍ line. When it comes before ⟍ word that begins with ⟍ consonant, this dot represents ⟍ very common word, as in " ⟍ page "; when it comes before ⟍ word that begins with ⟍ vowel, ⟍ dot represents another very common word, as in " ⟍ apple." No doubt you will have found it ⟍ easy matter ⟍ determine that ⟍ sign ⟍ expresses either " a " or " an."

⟍ next sign ⟍ small circle that ⟍ written on ⟍ line. It ⟍ written with ⟍ same motion that you use in writing ⟍ longhand letter O; that ⟍, in ⟍ direction indicated by this bent arrow ⟍ .   As you will have discovered, this small circle expresses " is." It ⟍ also used ⟍ express ⟍ word " his."

viii

.... signs ‿‿ two common words that are now introduced are somewhat similar ‿‿. appearance. These signs are called strokes. Each ‿...... them ..o........... shallow curve, written above ...... line. Each stroke ..o.... written from left ..\... right, but ..... stroke ‿‿ one word slopes downward, and ... . other stroke .o .. written ‿‿.... horizontal direction. ...... sign ‿‿. expresses " for," and ...... expresses " in." .... sign .‿. represents ., .. word " any " as well as " in." .‿‿... reading your shorthand notes there .o... never ‿‿.... difficulty ‿‿. knowing which word o... required because ., words before or after ...... sign ‿‿.... will always indicate whether it should be read as " in " or " any."

.... vertical straight stroke, written so that ..J.... rests on ...... ruled line, o.... introduced ..‿‿. this sentence. Write ..J.... lightly, ...'..... downward direction. .., next sign, ‹ , .o also written downwards, but above .., . line, and ...o.. only half as long as ...... stroke ...I... You will observe ..‹ .. this new sign .o .. curved. You will notice also ..‹... this curve .o.... thickened or " shaded." .'..... shaded stroke ...o... written with just .'. .. slightly heavier pressure on your pen or pencil. Light strokes like ..I.. and ‿‿.. are written without putting weight on .... pen; very little more pressure ...o.... needed ..\.... write .... shaded stroke.

.... last sign ‿‿... this series ...o...'..... short .... slanting dash, written .... upward direction, ... written above ...... line.

.... words which appear ‿‿.... shorthand ‿‿... this lesson occur so frequently ‿‿... all speech .'.... writing, .‿‿... form such ...'.... large percentage ‿‿... all ...,.... words used, ..‹... special signs are used ‿‿.... them. These special signs are called " Short Forms."

‿‿.. writing these short forms, make their length as nearly as possible ....,.... same as ...,.... signs printed .‿‿... this text. Observe carefully ....,..... differences ‿‿... length between ...'..... full-length stroke, ... half-length stroke, ...'.... dash.

ix

SUMMARY

...... following short forms have been used ...... this lesson:
...... to; ...... the; ...... of; ...... a/an; ...... is/his; ...... for;
...... in/any; ...... it; ...... that; ...... and.

PHRASING

When two or more ...... these common words follow each other,
...... signs ...... them may often be joined together ...... form ......
shorthand " phrase." ...... phrase saves time ...... writing, ... thus
increases speed. ...... phrase ...... formed only when ...... easy ......
clear joining can be made. ...... signs ...... would not join clearly,
...... therefore they are not phrased. Good examples ...... phrases
are ...... following:

...... of it, ... to it, ... for it, ... in it, ... it is, ... is it,
...... that is, ... is that, ... of that, ... to that, ... for that,
...... in that, ... and that, ... and for, ... and in, ... and is.

(The first sign in a phrase takes its right position with relation to
the line.)

...... form phrases, ... second sign ...... provided ...... " the."
This sign ...... short dash written as shown: ....
.... dash ...... " the " ...... joined only at ...... end
...... another sign; ...... never used standing alone, or at ...... beginning ...... phrase.

x

THE CONSONANT AND VOWEL SIGNS
OF PITMAN SHORTHAND

In Pitman Shorthand the word *pay* is expressed by the outline ⟍, a stroke for *p* and a dot for *ay*.

In shorthand writing a word is represented by a combination of signs, just as in longhand a word is spelled with a combination of letters. The signs used in shorthand to express consonants and vowels are much shorter and simpler than the longhand letters, and for this reason shorthand is written much faster than longhand.

Another reason for the speed of shorthand is that in shorthand the *sound* of a word is represented. In longhand the sounds that make up words are spelled in a great variety of ways.

For example, the vowel sound long $\overline{A}$ is spelled in eight different ways in the words *pay*, *they*, *rain*, *reign*, *weigh*, *break*, *same*, *gauge*. In Pitman Shorthand the vowel sound $\overline{A}$ is expressed by the single simple dot shown above. There is a simple sign for each of the sounds heard in English words.

The signs for five consonant sounds and for two vowel sounds are used in these shorthand outlines:

ape	pay	paid
Abe	bay	boat
ate	toe	tape
aid	day	date
apes	stay	soap

NOTE

The consonant strokes ⟍ *p* ⟍ *b* and ∣ *t* ∣ *d* are written downwards. They express two pairs of related sounds, a light stroke being used for a light sound and a heavier stroke for the corresponding heavier sound.

The S Circle .o.... is written with the motion usually used when writing the longhand letter ʻOʻ. It is thus joined on the right side of a straight downstroke: ⟋ soap, ⌐ stay, ⟋ₒ soaps, ⟋ₒ space.

When an outline has more than one consonant stroke, the strokes are joined without lifting the pen. The consonant strokes of an outline are written first, and then the vowel sign is placed.

A heavy point or dot, placed close to the middle of a stroke, expresses the long vowel sound $\bar{A}$: .·] aid, ..|·.. day, ..⌐.. stay.

A heavy dash, placed close to the middle of a stroke, expresses the long vowel sound $\bar{O}$: ..|⁻.. toe, ⁻|.. oats, ..⟋.. soap.

A vowel sign placed on the left side of a stroke is read before the stroke: ⟍.. ape, ⁻] .. oat, ⟋ soap.

A vowel sign placed on the right side of a stroke is read after the stroke: ⟍.. pay, ⟍ .. boat, ⟍ₒ.. space.

When the vowel sign $\bar{A}$ or $\bar{O}$ comes between two strokes it is placed after the first stroke and read after the first stroke: ⟍.. paid, ..|·. date, ⟍.. boat.

Two light dashes under an outline indicate a proper name: ..⟍.. Abe.

The following special punctuation signs are used in shorthand:
Shorthand: x   ꝑ   x   =   ↩   { }
Longhand: .   ?   !   -   —   ( )
            Period Question Exclamation Hyphen Dash Parenthesis
Other signs are written as in longhand.

LESSONS ONE TO FIFTY

LESSON ONE

CONSONANTS AND VOWELS

Straight Downstrokes: S Circle: Long Vowels Ā and Ō.

Sign	Letter	Name	Examples					
＼	P	*pee*	＼ ape	＼ pay	＼ pays/pace			
＼	B	*bee*	＼ Abe	＼ bay	＼ bays/base			
｜	T	*tee*	｜ ate	｜ toe	｜ toes			
｜	D	*dee*	｜ aid	｜ day	｜ dates			
｡	S	*ess circle*	oats	soap	stays			

S Circle expresses the sound of either S or. Z.

SHORT FORMS

to	for	be
of	in/any	to be
a/an	it	put
the	that	do
is/his	and	had/dollar
		I/eye
		you

The Short Forms in these two columns are used on pages viii–xii.

S Circle may be added to Short Forms: its, dollars.

PHRASES

today, to do, to you, of you, for you,
that you, and I, to be the, I had, I do,
I put, do you, to stay, in any, is to be.

EXERCISE ONE

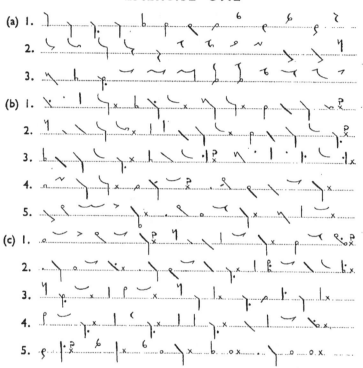

(a) 1.

2.

3.

(b) 1.

2.

3.

4.

5.

(c) 1.

2.

3.

4.

5.

(d) 1. The boat is in-that bay today. Is-that his boat? It-is his boat.

2. You had a dollar and-I-had a dollar. That-is for-you.

3. You paid for-the soap. I-put it in-the boat for-you.

4. Is any of-it in-the boat? You paid a dollar for-it.

5. Put-the soap and-the dates in-the boat that-is in-the bay.

LESSON TWO

CONSONANTS: Curved Downstrokes.

Sign	Letter	Name	Examples			
ٸ	F	*eff*	ٛ fade		ٮ face	
ٮ	V	*vee*	ٮ vote		ٮ save	
(	TH	*ith*	ٷ both		ٸ faith	
(	TH	*thee*	ٷ they		ٷ bathe	

S Circle is written inside curves.

OUTLINE DRILL

SAFE ٮ ٮ *   SAVE ٮ ٮ

FAITH ٷ ٷ   BATHE ٷ ٷ

VOTE ٷ ٷ   FADE ٷ ٷ

SHORT FORMS

....ٮ.... have   ....ٷ.... this   ....ٷ.... we

....(.... think   ....ٷ.... this is   ٷ all

....(.... them   ....ٮ.... several   ٷ .... ought/awe

The Short Form ٷ .. *we* is written upwards.

PHRASES

ٷ.. I have, ٷ we have, ٷ .. to have, ٷ.. I think, ٷ.. we think, ٷ. we had, ٷ. we do, ٷ.. they had, ٷ.. they do, ٷ.. for several, ٷ.... of them, ٷ .. to save, ٷ .. that this, ٷ.. for this, ..ٷ.. is this, ٷ........ all that is, ..ٷ.. ought to be.

* Related outlines are shown without a longhand key.

EXERCISE TWO

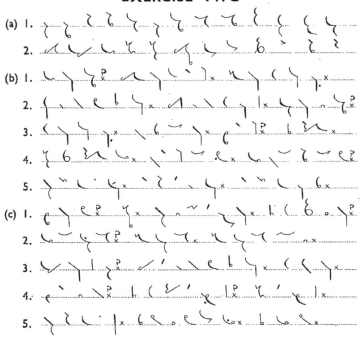

(d) 1. I-have-had to put it in-the safe. It-is all for-them.

2. We-have put several dollars in-that safe. We-have faith in-them.

3. Is-the boat in? We-think that-this-is-the boat. This-is it.

4. I-think that-we ought to vote for-this. You both ought to vote.

5. Have-we paid them to-do this? They ought-to-be paid to-do it.

6. Have-you any soap? This-is all-the face soap we-have.

LESSON THREE

CONSONANTS: Horizontal Strokes.

Sign	Letter	Name	Examples	
⟶	K	*kay*	case	sake
⟶	G	*gay*	gay	game
⌢	M	*em*	may	same
⌢	N	*en*	no/know	names
⌣	NG	*ing*	taking	making

A vowel sign placed above a horizontal stroke is read before the stroke.

A vowel sign placed underneath a horizontal stroke is read after the stroke.

S Circle is written on the upper side of a straight horizontal stroke.

OUTLINE DRILL

MAY

TAKE

CAME

NAME

NO/KNOW

SHORT FORM DERIVATIVES

being, doing, having.

PHRASES

doing the, I know, to take, we may, you may have, it may be, in this case.

EXERCISE THREE

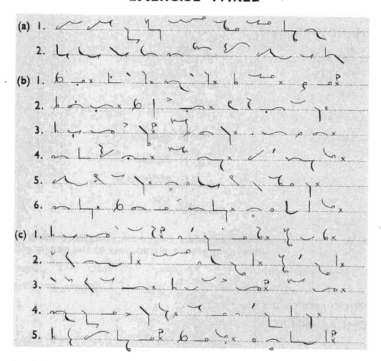

(d) 1. You-may-have this. I-know-the name of-the boat. Its name is "The May."

2. Take-this case of soap to-the boat that-is in-the bay. Take-it today.

3. Both you and-I ought to know-the day and-the date of-the game.

4. May is making this-case for-you. May is doing-that today.

5. It-may-be for-you. Is-that in-this-case? It-is being put in-that case.

LESSON FOUR

VOWELS: Short Vowels Ĕ and Ŭ.

OUTLINE DRILL

(a) SET ..f.. b̤̣   GET ⌐ ⌐b

     SAID .f..   ENOUGH ⌐L

     DEBT ..|.. |..

     SENSE ௳ ௳

(b) DOES b̤   SUNDAY ⌐1

     UP ⋋   MONDAY ⌐⌐1

     SUM/SOME ⌐   MONTH ⌐(⌐b

     SUN/SON ௳   UN- ⌐1 ⌐

     SUPPOSE ℅

The short vowel Ĕ is expressed by a light dot; the short vowel Ŭ by a light dash. These vowel signs are placed close to the middle of a consonant stroke. Compare: |· *date*, ·| *debt*; b̤ *dose*, b̤ *does*. In such outlines as ⌐1 *get*, ⌐1 *Sunday*, the first downstroke rests on the line.

SHORT FORMS

...... ° ..... as/has, ... ' on, ...|... but, ..|.... he, ⌐⌐ manufacture / manufactured.

PHRASES

⌐1 on Sunday, ℅ as/has the, ρ is he, ' on the, ⌐ to get the.

The dash for *the* is written upward when a sharper angle is thus obtained: ⌐1 get the, b̤ set the.

The signs for *on* and *but* are slanted to form the phrases ' *on the*, ...b.... *but the*.

EXERCISE FOUR

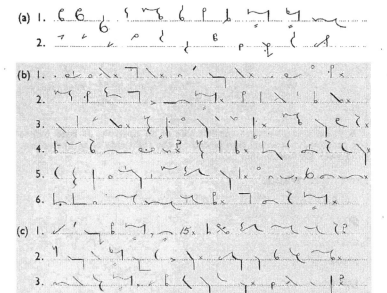

(d) 1. You-may-have to-make-them get it for-you. I-have-several sets.

2. May said that-he ought to-get enough for all of-them.

3. I-have-had this for-several months. Has-he manufactured enough sets?

4. You-may get some of-them on-Sunday and some on-Monday.

5. I-know-that-he said that-the case is on-the boat.

LESSON FIVE

CONSONANTS: Upstrokes

Sign	Letter	Name	Examples	
_/C_	L	*el*	_/C_ less	_⌢_ length
_/_	W	*way*	_/_ way/weigh	_⌢_ Wednesday
_/_	Y	*yay*	_/_ yes	_⌢_ yellow

A vowel sign placed on the left side of an upstroke is read before the consonant: a vowel sign placed on the right side of an upstroke is read after the consonant.

OUTLINE DRILL

SALE/SAIL

SELL

SELF

LOW

LOVE

COAL

MAIL

DETAIL

WAY/WEIGH

DELAY

PHRASES

you will, you will be, I hope, we hope.

In a phrase, the word *will* is expressed by the stroke L; the word *hope* is expressed by the stroke P.

EXERCISE FIVE

(a) 1. [shorthand outlines]

    2. [shorthand outlines]

(b) 1. [shorthand outlines]

    2. [shorthand outlines]

    3. [shorthand outlines]

    4. [shorthand outlines]

    5. [shorthand outlines]

(c) 1. [shorthand outlines]

    2. [shorthand outlines]

    3. [shorthand outlines]

    4. [shorthand outlines]

    5. [shorthand outlines]

    6. [shorthand outlines]

(d) 1. I-hope-you-will mail it to-them today. I-have sold less of-this today.

    2. I-have some of-the details. They-will mail them to-you on-Wednesday.

    3. Have-you sold any of-this below a dollar a length? I-have sold this.

    4. They-may-be slow but I-have faith in-them. Yes, I-have sold it to-them.

    5. I-hope-you-will put this on sale today. Is-that-the way to-manufacture it?

LESSON SIX

DOUBLE-CONSONANT SIGNS

⟍ play, ⟍ able, ⌐ close, ⊢ total, ⌐ settle.

The hook for L is written on the same side of a stroke as the S Circle: ⟍ pl, ⟍ bl, ⌠ tl, ⌠ dl, ⌐ kl, ⌐ gl.

These double-consonant strokes are called PEL, BEL, etc.

S Circle, coming before the double-consonant strokes ⟍⌠ etc., is written inside the hook: ⌠ settle.

OUTLINE DRILL

PLAY ⟍ ⟍ ⟍

ABLE ⟍ ⟍ ⟍ ⊢ ⊢

CLOSE ⌐ ⌐ ⌐ ⌐

CLAIM ⌐ ⌐ ⌐

CLOTHE ⊓ ⊔ ⊏

TOTAL ⊢ ⊢

COUPLE ⊓ ⊐

SHORT FORMS

⎯ can	⌣ thing	⌣ anything
⎯ come	⌠ {deliver / delivered / delivery}	⌣ nothing
⎯ go	⟍ {believe / believed / belief}	⌣ something
⎯ give/given		⎯ going

PHRASES

⟍ to give, ⟍ to go, ⌐ you can, ⟍ to deliver.

The vowel sign is always written in the phrase ⟍ *to go*, to distinguish it from ⟍ *to give*.

EXERCISE SIX

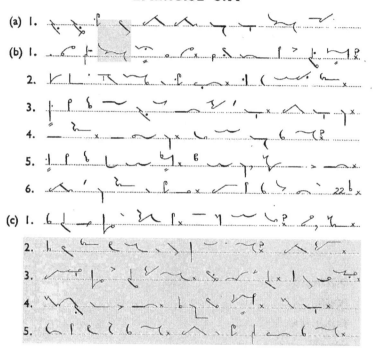

(a) 1.

(b) 1.

2.

3.

4.

5.

6.

(c) 1.

2.

3.

4.

5.

(d) 1. Can-we give-them any details of-the delivery dates?

    2. I-have put several of-the sets on-the table for-them.

    3. We-believe that-you-can come up for-the things on-Monday.

    4. Do-you think that-you-can settle-the claim this month?

    5. We-believe that-we-have to-go to-that place today.

    6. I-have given-them a couple of-the sets. We-can deliver nothing
       today.

LESSON SEVEN

CONSONANTS: Two Forms for R

Sign	Letter	Name	Examples			
⟋	R	*ray*	⟋ red		⟋ race/raise	
⟍	R	*ar*	⟋ air		⟍ force	

When R begins a word use RAY ⟋ (an upstroke); when R ends a word use AR ⟍ (a downstroke). Compare: ⟋ ray, ⟋ air.

OUTLINE DRILL

RACE/RAISE ⟋ ⟋

RED ⟋ ⟋ ⟋

ROAD ⟋ ⟋

AIR ⟋ ⟋

SIR ⟋ ⟋

DOOR ⟋ ⟋

FOUR ⟋ ⟋

FAIR/FARE ⟋ ⟋

COLOR ⟋ ⟋

REPAIR ⟋ ⟋

SHORT FORMS

⟋ are, ⟋ our/hour, ⟋ your, ⟋ with, ⟋ too/two, ⟋ manufacturer.

PHRASES

⟋ we are, ⟋ are we, ⟋ to our, ⟋ to your, ⟋ for your, ⟋ with the, ⟋ with it, ⟋ two hours.

EXERCISE SEVEN

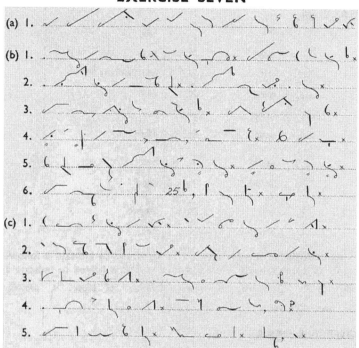

(d) 1. Do-you believe that-you-can make-the repairs in four hours?

2. The totals of all-the claims are given, with-the names and-the dates.

3. We-are going to-the race. Ted is going with Ray, too.

4. We-are to-be "on-the air" today. We-can raise this sum.

5. We-hope-that-the manufacturers can make-the repairs for-you.

6. Is your door the same color as our door? It-is red.

LESSON EIGHT

HALVING

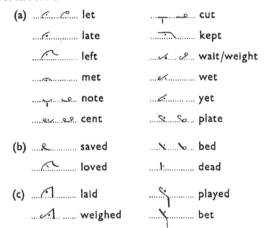

(a) let   cut

late   kept

left   wait/weight

met   wet

note   yet

cent   plate

(b) saved   bed

loved   dead

(c) laid   played

weighed   bet

In a one-syllable word a light stroke is halved to indicate a following T. In a one-syllable word a shaded stroke is halved to indicate a following D. Compare: *late*, *laid*; *plate*, *played*, *bed*, *bet*.

OUTLINE DRILL

MAY

WAY/WEIGH

SAVE

LOVE

BAY

PHRASES

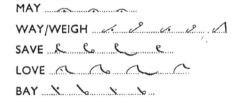

to let, too late, I note, I have saved.

EXERCISE EIGHT

(a) 1.

(b) 1.

2.

3.

4.

5.

6.

(c) 1.

2.

3.

4.

5.

(d) 1. You ought to-make a note of all-that-you have-saved.

2. As-the day is fair we-can wait for-you. Is-it too-late?

3. It-is too-late to-make a claim. Have-they left yet?

4. You-may-be kept up late. You-will-be kept waiting.

5. The weights are given in-that table. I-have cut it in two.

6. We-note that-you paid two cents. I loved-the game.

LESSON NINE

HALVING

꒦ꞁ noted	꒦꒛ method
꒦ꞁ waited	꒦ effected
꒦ settled	꒦ result
꒦ selected	꒦ doesn't

In a word that has more than one syllable, a stroke is halved to indicate that it is followed by either T or D.

OUTLINE DRILL

NOTE
RELATE
RESULT
WAIT

SHORT FORMS

me	should	could
when	sent	without
special/specially	quite	{ build building able to

PHRASES

for me,   when the,   you should,   could be, let me know,   to build,   able to.

Note the use of halving to express the word *to* in the phrase ꒦ *able to.*

EXERCISE NINE

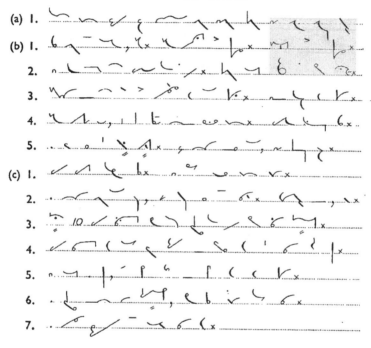

(a) 1.

(b) 1.

2.

3.

4.

5.

(c) 1.

2.

3.

4.

5.

6.

7.

(d) 1. You-should-have waited in-the building. We waited for two-hours.

2. Let-me-know when-the results are sent to-May.

3. We-have-had to-go without them. We-have noted your methods.

4. As you sent-the case on-Monday, we should-have it today. The claim ought-to-be settled.

5. We should-have-sent it to-you when-it came in. We-have-sent several special sets to-you.

LESSON TEN

CONSONANTS: Downstrokes

Sign	Letter	Name	Examples	
/ʒ/	CH	**chay**	⌐ such	∠ check
/	J	**jay**	⌐ age	⌐ page
)ʒ	S	**ess**	)⁻ so	⁻) us
)	Z	**zee**	)° zealous	) was (*Short Form*)
⌐	SH	**ish**	∧ show	∠ shape
)ʒ	ZH	**zhee**	⌐ usual (*Short Form*) ⌐ unusual	

Note the use of the stroke S in words like)· *say,*)⁻ *so,* ⁻) *us.* The stroke must be used in order to place the vowel sign.

OUTLINE DRILL

CHECK ∠ ∠ ∠ ∠
TOUCH)⁻))
AGE / / ∠ /
JUDGE /⁻ / ∠
CHANGE ∠ ∠ ∠ ∠
SHOW ∧ ∧ /
SAY)·) /·

SHORT FORMS

/ which,) was, ⌐ shall, ⌐ usual/usually, ⌐ knowledge.

PHRASES

) was the, ⌐ which was the, ⌐ in touch, ∠ we shall be, ∠ to such, ∠ · check the,) do so, ∠ which will.

EXERCISE TEN

(a) 1. [shorthand outlines]

2. [shorthand outlines]

(b) 1. [shorthand outlines]

2. [shorthand outlines]

3. [shorthand outlines]

4. [shorthand outlines]

5. [shorthand outlines]

(c) 1. [shorthand outlines]

2. [shorthand outlines]

3. [shorthand outlines]

4. [shorthand outlines]

5. [shorthand outlines]

6. [shorthand outlines]

(d) 1. Make a special note of anything which-should-be changed.

2. They-will take all-that we-are-able-to make specially for-them.

3. We checked the case as-usual when it-was in-the building.

4. I-know-that-he-has no knowledge of-this. I-shall-have to-check them, too.

5. I-hope-you-will get in-touch with me and-with-the manufacturers, as-usual.

LESSON ELEVEN

VOWELS: Short Vowel Ă and Long Vowel AH

(a) ....|.... at   ....L.... tax   ....⌒.... am

....ʹ|.... sat   ...⌁.... example   ....⌁.... among

....⌁.... pass   ....\\.... bad   ....⌁.... away

....⌒.... mass   ....⌁.... glad   ....⊤.... ago

(b) ....⌐.... car   ....⌁.... far   ....⌁.... afar

The short vowel Ă is expressed by a light dot; the long vowel AH is expressed by a heavy dot.

Ă and AH are called " First Place " Vowels, and the sign is written close to the beginning of a consonant stroke.

The vowels Ā, Ĕ, Ō, Ŭ, used in Exercises 1–10, are called " Second Place " Vowels.

When the first vowel in a word is a first place vowel, the outline is written in first position, that is, above the line. When the first vowel in a word is a second place vowel, the outline is written in second position, that is, on the line.

OUTLINE DRILL

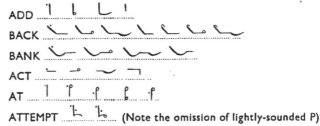

ADD ....⏋ ⌁ L ⌁....

BACK ....⌁ ⌁ ⌁ ⌁ ⌁ ⌁ ⌁....

BANK ....⌁ ⌁ ⌁ ⌁....

ACT ....⌁ ⌁ ⌁ ⌐....

AT ....| ʹ| ·ʹ| ʹ| ʹ|....

ATTEMPT ....⌁ ⌁.... (Note the omission of lightly-sounded P)

PHRASES

....⌁.... I shall be glad, ...⌁.... as far as, ...⌁.... in this way.

EXERCISE ELEVEN

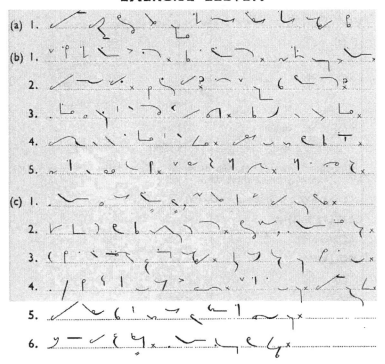

(d) 1. This-is a fair example. I-shall-be-glad to-go to-the building
for-you.

2. The case was put among-the things at-the back of-the car.

3. I-hope that-you-will-be-able-to show us a sample of-this in black.

4. Is-the car far away? It-is at-the back of-the bank.

5. I-paid-the tax a month ago. I-was glad to act for-you.

6. Add it up, and put it away in-the safe. It-is bad for-them to
attempt to-do this.

LESSON TWELVE

VOWELS: Short Vowel Ŏ and Long Vowel AW

(a) ⌐ off   ⌐ got   ⌐ lot

  ⌐ wrong   ⌐ or   ⌐ long

  ⌐ watch   ⌐ not   ⌐ follow

  ⌐ job   ⌐ loss   ⌐ follows

(b) ⌐ bought   ⌐ cause   ⌐ saw

  ⌐ law   ⌐ thought   ⌐ small

The short vowel Ŏ is expressed by a light dash; the long vowel
AW is expressed by a thick dash.

Ŏ and AW are first place vowels.

OUTLINE DRILL

LONG

FOLLOW

LOT

GOT

OR

NOT

LOSS

TALK

CAUSE

SMALL

PHRASES

 to watch,   too small,   I thought,   I saw,
 does not.

EXERCISE TWELVE

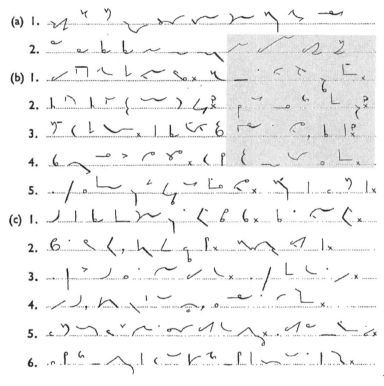

(a) 1.

2.

(b) 1.

2.

3.

4.

5.

(c) 1.

2.

3.

4.

5.

6.

(d) 1. The pages which I-have checked are-not to-be changed in-any-way.

2. We-thought it-was wrong when-we got it. It-was a long way.

3. The watch I-bought was smaller. I-thought I-saw you not long-ago.

4. We-hope that-we-are-not causing any delay. I-bought several of-the watches.

5. You have-sent-the wrong case. It-is-not-the case I-bought.

LESSON THIRTEEN

DIPHTHONG I

.......⌄.... by/buy, ...⌒.... wise, ...⌒⌃.... life, ...⌒⌝.... wide.

The sign ....⌄.... is used for the diphthong sound ī. It is written in the first vowel place.

OUTLINE DRILL

BY/BUY ....

DIE ....

MY ....

LIKE ....

TIME ....

LIGHT ....

SIGN ....

FIRE ....

LIFE ....

DESIRE ....

SUPPLY ....

REPLY ....

SIDE ....

SIZE ....

WRITING ....

SOMETIMES ....

PHRASES

.... in time/any time, ... two miles, ... to sign.

EXERCISE THIRTEEN

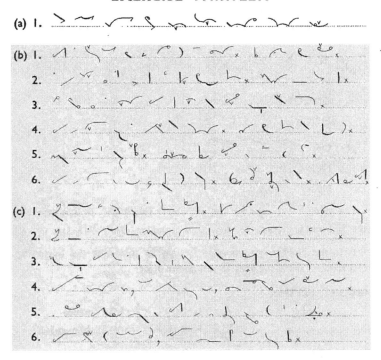

(a) I.

(b) I.

2.

3.

4.

5.

6.

(c) I.

2.

3.

4.

5.

6.

(d) 1. The plates which-you have delivered are-not-the same as-the plates you supplied several months ago, and we-have-sent them back.

2. The car should-not-be on-this side of-the road. The road is wide.

3. I-have-not yet had a reply to-my note, but we-are writing to-them today.

4. Do-you desire to buy a supply of-the signs in-this size?

LESSON FOURTEEN

DIPHTHONG OI

OUTLINE DRILL

(a) BOY

VOICE

EMPLOY

ENJOY

(b) OIL

ITEM

NIGHT

The sign is used for the diphthong sound OI. It is written in the first vowel place: *boy*, *employ*.

Both the diphthong signs I and OI may be joined at the beginning of a stroke. Note the special outline for *night*:

SHORT FORMS

who | January | never
much | February | November

PHRASES

I will, I can, I am, I read, I believe/d, I like, too much, so much.

Phrases may be formed by using only the first half of the Short Form I.

The full outline for *much* is used to form the phrases *too much*, *so much*.

EXERCISE FOURTEEN

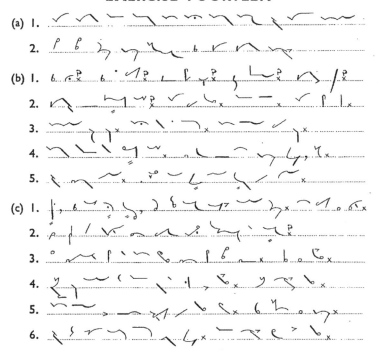

(a) 1.

2.

(b) 1.

2.

3.

4.

5.

(c) 1.

2.

3.

4.

5.

6.

(d) 1. I-enclose some cuttings of-several items which I-read in " The.
Times."

2. I-enjoyed them so-much when I-read them that I-thought you
might enjoy them too.

3. In both January and-February we sell four times as-much oil as
in November.

4. Do-you know of any boys who are-not employed?

5. I-believe I-can employ-the boy. I-will buy-the oil for-you.

LESSON FIFTEEN

S CIRCLE MEDIALLY: Ray Medially

OUTLINE DRILL

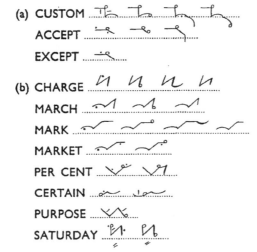

(a) CUSTOM

ACCEPT

EXCEPT

(b) CHARGE

MARCH

MARK

MARKET

PER CENT

CERTAIN

PURPOSE

SATURDAY

S Circle is written outside of an angle formed by two straight strokes.

In the middle of an outline *Ray* ⟋ is generally used.

SHORT FORMS

⌐ why   ⌐ exchange/exchanged

⟋ yesterday   ⟋ expect/expected

PHRASES

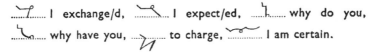

I exchange/d,   I expect/ed,   why do you, why have you,   to charge,   I am certain.

EXERCISE FIFTEEN

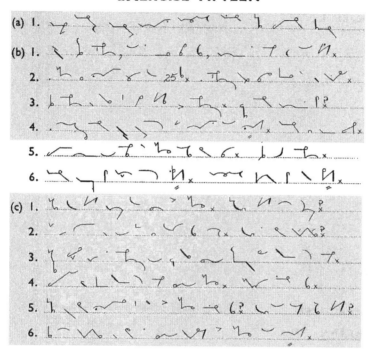

(d) 1. I-had expected them to-come in March, but–they could-not come.

2. We-have added our usual mark-up of 25 per cent.

3. We accepted the customer's note for-the unpaid items.

4. All except two of-the boys can-be employed. Are they quite certain?

5. I-expected you to-make-this exchange yesterday, not on-Saturday.

LESSON SIXTEEN

STEE LOOP

.·*?*.. state, ..*e*... west, ...⌐... must, ..*b*·... just, ..⤵.. best.

A small loop (called STEE) expresses the sound ST or ZD. It is written in the same direction as the S Circle.

OUTLINE DRILL

(a) STOP ....

    STEP ....

    STORE ....

    STONE ....

(b) TEST ....

    LAST ....

    SUGGEST ....

    REST ....

    WASTE ....

    COST ....

    AUGUST ....

(c) TAX ....

    PASS ....

    BASE ....

    FACE ....

S Circle after STEE Loop is written as shown. Note the medial use of STEE Loop in such outlines as .. *testing*, .. *suggesting*.

SHORT FORMS

..*o*.... first, ...⤴... next, ..⌐.. most.

Note the distinguishing outlines: ..⊓.. *caused*, ..⌐.. *cost*.

EXERCISE SIXTEEN

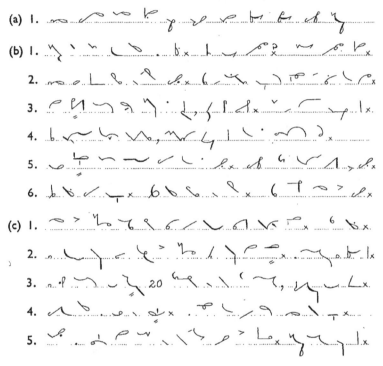

(a) 1.

(b) 1.

2.

3.

4.

5.

6.

(c) 1.

2.

3.

4.

5.

(d) 1. Last night the judge said that-he believed-the law was quite · just.

2. They state that-the suggested change in-the law was-not passed.

3. It-was lost by several votes. I-have kept this item in stock.

4. As I-pass-the store on-my way, I-can stop in for-you.

5. I suggest that-it might be best for-you to-wait for a day or-two.

6. Most of-the loss is caused by waste, and-this must stop.

LESSON SEVENTEEN

SEZ CIRCLE: STER LOOP

(a) .... causes .... passes .... faces .... success

(b) .... master .... waster .... tester .... masters

The sound SES, SEZ, or ZEZ at the end of a word is expressed by a large circle (called SEZ).

The sound STER at the end of a word is expressed by a large loop (called STER).

These Circles and Loops are written in the same direction as S Circle.

OUTLINE DRILL

MASS ....

PLACE ....

CASE ....

PASS ....

PURPOSE ....

LOSS ....

SUCCESS ....

WAYS ....

Final S Circle after SEZ Circle or STER Loop is written as shown.

SHORT FORMS

.... would, ... because, ... themselves/this is, ... those, ... ourselves, ... myself.

Note the Special Outlines: .... also, ... always, ... almost.

PHRASES

.... with those, ... those who, ... because of.

EXERCISE SEVENTEEN

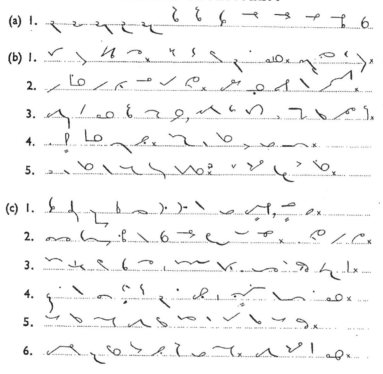

(d) 1. They themselves believe-that nothing is wrong with-the car.

2. They state that when-they deliver a car they always check it first.

3. They also give it a road test. A test is given in all cases.

4. We-have ourselves given those-cases away to-the boys.

5. We-shall master it because we-desire to-have success.

6. The faces of-the boys show us that-they-have met with success.

LESSON EIGHTEEN
DOUBLE-CONSONANT SIGNS

......⟨..... brought, ...⌐°.... across, ...ˇ₁.... better, ...⌐ᐟ.... October.

The hook for R is written on the opposite side of a stroke to the S Circle: ...⟍.. pr, ...⟍.. br, ...⌐.. tr, ...⌐.. dr, ...⌐.. chr, ...⌐... jr, ...⌐.. kr, ...⌐.. gr.

These double-consonant strokes are called PER, BER, etc.

OUTLINE DRILL

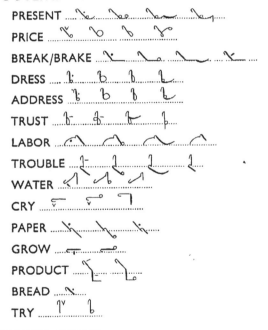

PRESENT
PRICE
BREAK/BRAKE
DRESS
ADDRESS
TRUST
LABOR
TROUBLE
WATER
CRY
PAPER
GROW
PRODUCT
BREAD
TRY

SHORT FORMS

....⟍.... probable/probably, ...⌐.... danger, ...⌐... dangerous.

EXERCISE EIGHTEEN

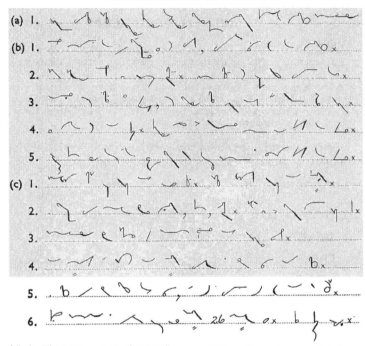

(a) 1.

(b) 1.

2.

3.

4.

5.

(c) 1.

2.

3.

4.

5.

6.

(d) 1. The papers state that at-the present-time the water supply is low.

2. We market products that-we grow ourselves. It-is better to-take this trouble.

3. I-am going to-try to-go across to-the West late in October.

4. I-think it-would probably be better to-try to-make-this bread ourselves.

5. They themselves brought-the dresses. I-trust that-the prices are low.

6. It-is better at-present not to-try. They broke up-the cases which they brought with-them.

LESSON NINETEEN

VOWEL: Long Ē

...∫... each, ...∫... she, ...(... these, ...ℓ. least, ...ℓ. steel/steal.

The long vowel Ē is expressed by a heavy dot written close to the end of a stroke. Ē is called a " third place " vowel. When the first vowel in a word is third place, the outline is written in the third position, that is, through the line.

When a third place vowel comes between two strokes the sign is written in front of the second stroke: ...∫... reach, ...⌒.. meal.

Compare: ...⌐⌐... far ...⌐⌐ fare ...⌐⌐ fear.

OUTLINE DRILL

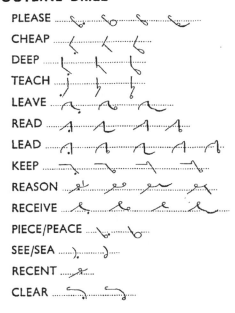

PLEASE

CHEAP

DEEP

TEACH

LEAVE

READ

LEAD

KEEP

REASON

RECEIVE

PIECE/PEACE

SEE/SEA

RECENT

CLEAR

EXERCISE NINETEEN

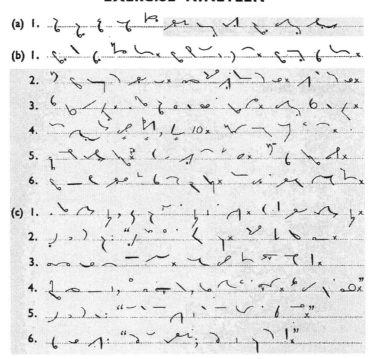

(a) 1.

(b) 1.

2.

3.

4.

5.

6.

(c) 1.

2.

3.

4.

5.

6.

(d) 1. The purpose of-the talk was-not clear to-me. I-see no reason for-it.

2. I-fear I-shall-not-have time to-read any but-the most recent pieces of-writing.

3. Most of-the oil was delivered last night. Have-you had a meal?

4. Your recent note stated that-the steel cases would reach me on-Saturday.

5. The water in-the-sea is deep. I-shall keep these pieces for-you.

LESSON TWENTY

VOWEL: Short Ĭ

 ...ᴗ... if, ...ᶠ... sit, ...ᵖ... list, ...ᴶ... ship, ...ᶠ... still.

The short vowel Ĭ is expressed by a light dot written close to the end of a stroke. Ĭ is a third place vowel.

OUTLINE DRILL

(a) SIT ...ᶠ... ᶠ...

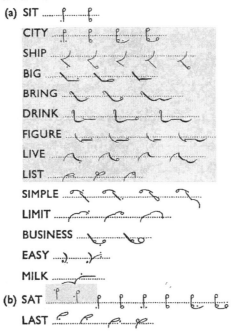

CITY ...ᶠ... ᶠ... ᶠ... ᶠ...

SHIP ...

BIG ...

BRING ...

DRINK ...

FIGURE ...

LIVE ...

LIST ...

SIMPLE ...

LIMIT ...

BUSINESS ...

EASY ...

MILK ...

(b) SAT ...ᶠ... ᶠ... ᶠ... ᶠ... ᶠ... ᶠ... ᶠ...

LAST ...ᵖ... ᵖ... ᵖ... ᵖ...

PHRASES

...ᴗ... to us, ...ᴗ... of us, ...ᴗ... for us, ...ᶜ... with us, ...ᴖ. give us.

S circle is used to express " *us* " in a phrase.

EXERCISE TWENTY

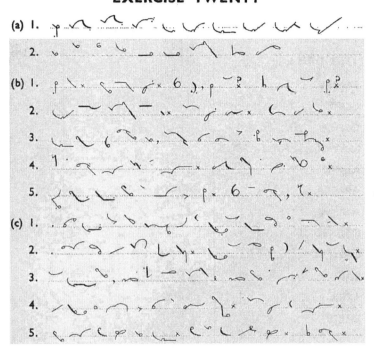

(a) 1.
2.

(b) 1.
2.
3.
4.
5.

(c) 1.
2.
3.
4.
5.

(d) 1. Is-the water deep enough for-the big ships? Drink lots of-water.

2. I-think myself it-would-be simpler to-make a list, and give it to-us.

3. We should like to-exchange this, if-we-may. The milk is bad.

4. If-you-will give-us the names, we-can easily make a list of-them.

5. Ship-the cases to-us in-the cheapest way with-the least delay.

6. The steel has-not yet reached our city. I-must set a limit on-the sum to-be paid.

LESSON TWENTY-ONE

SHORT VOWEL Ĭ, Continued

⌇ clearly, ⌇ wisely, ⌇ family, ⌇ office.

When there is more than one vowel sign in an outline, it is the first vowel sign that decides the position of the outline.

OUTLINE DRILL

(a) FAMILY

COPY

OFFICE

SERVICE

AGREE

APPEAR

ANIMAL

DEGREE

CAPITAL

BABY

APRIL

CREDIT

(b) MONTH   SAFE

BAD   NAME

LIGHT   LATE

LIKE   DAY

PHRASES

⌇ you will agree with, ⌇ I agree that.

EXERCISE TWENTY-ONE

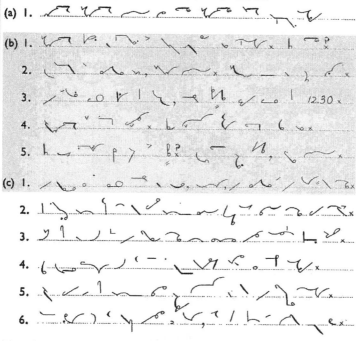

(d) 1. I-must come back to-the city in April. It-is our custom to-give a month's credit.

2. It appears likely that-they-will-agree to-make copies monthly.

3. I-have-not met them lately, but it appears likely that-they-will-agree.

4. We-can safely expect a better service. Have-you put any capital in-the business?

5. I-have bought this small animal to-give to-the baby.

6. All-the family agreed that-the service should-be copied in-this city.

LESSON TWENTY-TWO

VOWELS: Short O͞O and Long O͞O

.... took, ... book, ... food, ... poor.

The short vowel O͞O is expressed by a light dash, and the long vowel O͞O by a heavy dash. Both O͞O and O͞O are third place vowels.

OUTLINE DRILL

(a) BOOK ....

     LOOK ....

     PULL ....

     FULLY ....

     INTO ....

(b) MOVE ....

     USE ....

     TRUE ....

     BLUE ....

     JULY ....

SHORT FORMS

.... what	.... different/difference	.... him
.... wish	.... dear	.... himself
.... wished	.... during	

PHRASES

.... what is, ... Dear Sir, ... Yours truly, ... to him.

The vowel is always written in such phrases as .... *to him*, ... *to himself*, to distinguish the forms from .... *to me*, ... *to myself*.

EXERCISE TWENTY-TWO

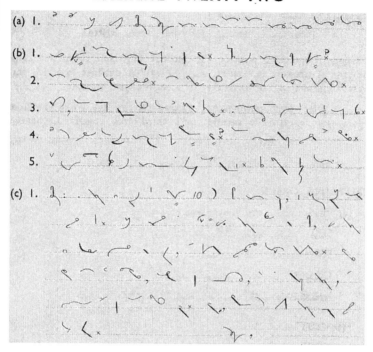

(d) 1. I suggest that-you look into-the cause of-the trouble for-him.

2. I-wish I could say what-is causing these poor results.

3. The poor results are caused in no small degree by-the methods you use.

4. I-took-the book to-him. It gives much food for thought.

5. During July and August I-wish him to-look fully into our methods.

6. I-know-that-he said himself that-he uses these two books.

LESSON TWENTY-THREE

THIRD PLACE VOWELS

....ᷝ.... since, ...ᷝ.... soon, ... l..... did, ...⌒.... written.

There is no third position for outlines in which there are only horizontal strokes: ..ᷝ.. seen, ____. king; or outlines in which the first upstroke or downstroke is a half-length stroke: ....l.... did,

....ᷝ.... little. Such outlines are written on the line when the first vowel sign is either a second or a third place vowel. Compare:

....⌒.... mat, ..ᷤ.. met, ..⌒.. meet; ...⌒.... among, ..⌒⌒.. money,

____. king; ..ᷝ.... lightly, ...ᷝ.. lately, ...ᷝ.... little.

OUTLINE DRILL

(a) MISS ....ᷤ....ᷤ....ᷤ....⌒....

SIX ....ᷤ....ᷤ....ᷤ....

SEEM ..ᷤ:....ᷤ....⌒....

GOOD ....⌐....ᷤ....ᷤ....⌐....

INCREASE ..ᷤ....ᷤ....ᷤ....ᷤ....

(b) FOOT ....∪....∪....

EAST ....∫...

SYSTEM ...ᷤᷤ...

INDEED ....⌐l...

NEEDED ...⌐l....

MOVED ....⌐....

PHRASES

..ᷤ... it seems, .⌒⌒ᷤ six months, ..⌒ᷤ.. we have seen, ..ᷤ... it may seem.

EXERCISE TWENTY-THREE

(a) 1.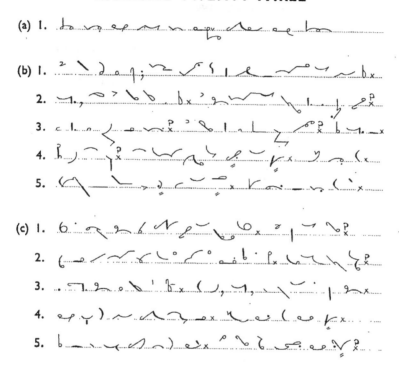

(b) 1.

2.

3.

4.

5.

(c) 1.

2.

3.

4.

5.

(d) 1. Dear-Sir: The price of steel has increased so-much during-the last six-months that-we-believe we ourselves shall soon be forced to increase-the price of almost all of-our products. To-meet-the increases in costs, it-seems likely that our charges for-some products may go up as-much-as two cents a foot. We-believe it-would-be wise for-you to buy without delay some of-the items which-will-be needed in-your business, since most of-the goods you use can-be supplied today at little or no added cost to-you. Our most recent price-list is enclosed. Yours-truly,

LESSON TWENTY-FOUR

DIPHTHONGS Ū AND OW

...ꞁ... Tuesday, ...ᘰ... few, ...ρ... south, ...ʜ... doubt, ...ᴎ... about.

The sign. ...ᴖ... is used to express the diphthong sound Ū, and the sign ...ʌ.... to express the diphthong sound OW. ...ᴖ.... and ....ʌ... are third place signs. They may be joined at the end of a stroke when a convenient joining is possible. ...ᴖ... may be turned on its side to obtain a convenient joining, as in ᘰꞈ value. Strokes with a joined diphthong at the end may be halved for either T or D, as ..ʜ.. doubt.

OUTLINE DRILL

(a) ISSUE ...ᴊ........ᴊ... ...ᴣ... .

     VIEW ...ᘰ...... ᘰ.........ᘰᴎ ...

     NEW ....ᴖᴄ... ...ᴖᴘ.......ᴖᴣ......... ᴖᴣ........

     OUT ....ᴊ..........ᴼᴾ...

     ANNOUNCE ....

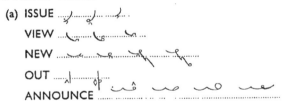

(b) BUY ....

     BOY .....

     EMPLOY ....

     POWER ....

     FEW .....

     VALUE .....

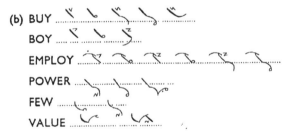

A small dash is added to a diphthong sign to express a following vowel. This sign is called a Triphone.

SHORT FORM

    ....ʌ.... how

CONTRACTED FORM

    .ᴖᴎ. now

EXERCISE TWENTY-FOUR

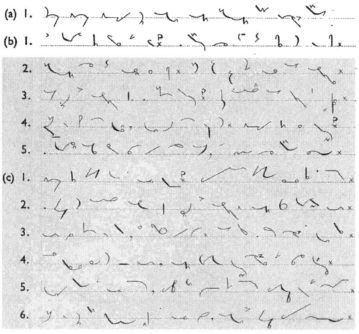

(d) 1. When I-received-the news about-the new issue I-got in-touch with him.

2. We-have-no-doubt that-this might be a wise move, but our powers are limited.

3. I-expect to-leave for-the South on Tuesday to see my new employer.

4. In-view of-these changes we should think about issuing a new list.

5. I-wish you would show me how to-bring out this new issue.

6. How-can-they take-the books with-them? They-have-no value now.

LESSON TWENTY-FIVE

SIGNS FOR H

Sign	Letter	Name	Examples
	H	**Upward Hay**	happy head heat
	H	**Downward Hay**	he high higher
	H	**Dash (or Tick) Hay**	home whole hear/here

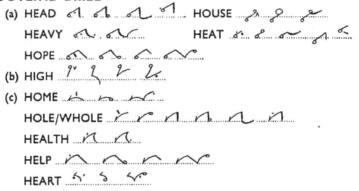

Upward Hay is generally used. Downward Hay is used when H is the only consonant sound in a word, and in words beginning with *high*. Dash Hay is used before M, L and R.

OUTLINE DRILL

(a) HEAD   HOUSE

HEAVY   HEAT

HOPE

(b) HIGH

(c) HOME

HOLE/WHOLE

HEALTH

HELP

HEART

In a few cases H may be omitted, or expressed by a dot, as: ...... *perhaps*, ... *household*.

PHRASES

...... **to hear**, ... **for whom**, ... **he is**.

Note that the Short Form ...... *he is* used only in the middle or at the end of a phrase: ...... *he can*, ... *that he can*, ... *if he*.

EXERCISE TWENTY-FIVE

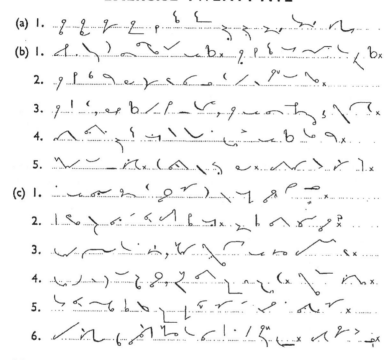

(d) 1. The teacher about whom I-talked to-you has written a new book.

2. Her book is reviewed in today's newspaper, and-the reviewer thinks highly of-it.

3. I-am indeed happy to-hear-the good news about your new house.

4. I-never had any doubt that-the manufacturer would go ahead with-it.

5. Perhaps I-can help in some-way. If so, I-hope-you-will let-me-know.

6. At-the head of-the page place-the date; at-the foot, sign your name.

LESSON TWENTY-SIX

DOUBLE-CONSONANTS: Curves

...ᒪ... ever, ...(..... either, ...ᔕ... Friday, ...|..... differ,
....ᐸᵛ.. fly, ᐳᶜ... final, ...ᐳ..... beautiful, ...ᐟᐷ... hopeful,
..ᐟᐳ.... summer, ...ᐁᐳ.... sooner, ...ᔕ..... safer.

A small hook, written at the beginning of a curved stroke, forms
the double-consonants FR, VR, etc. ᔕ.. fr, ᔕ.. vr, ᒪ.. thr,
..ᒪ.. THr, ...ᔎ.. shr, ...ᔎ.. zhr, ᐸᐳ. mr, ᐁᐟ. nr, as: ᐟᒪ.. *offer*,
ᐳ. *measure*.

A large hook, written at the beginning of a curved stroke, forms the
double-consonants FL, VL, etc. ᔕ.. fl, ᔕ.. vl, ..ᒪ... thl, ᐸᐳ ml,
ᐁᒪ.. nl, as: ᐸᐷ *flying*, ..ᐸᐷ... *helpful*.

S Circle, coming before the double-consonants ..ᔕᔕ... etc., is
written inside the hook: ..ᐟᐳ.... *summer*, ...ᐁᐳ.... *sooner*.

OUTLINE DRILL

(a) EVER ..ᔕ ᔕ..   (b) FLY ᐸᵛ ᐸ ᐸᵧ
    OFFER ᐟᒪ ᒪᵧ   DEVELOP ᒡ ᒡ
    OTHER ᐟᒪ ᒪᵧ   POWERFUL ᐳ ᐳ
    DIFFER ..|.....|.....   (c) SUMMER ᐟᐳ ᐟᐳ
    MEASURE ...ᐳ ᐳ..   SAFER ᔕ
    EFFORT ..ᒪ ᒪᵧ..   SOONER ᐁᐳ

SHORT FORMS

....|..... advertise/advertised/advertisement, ᐁᐳ.. govern/governed.

SHORT FORM DERIVATIVE

..ᔕᐳ.. everything.

EXERCISE TWENTY-SIX

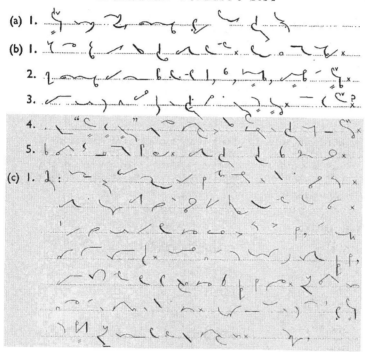

(a) 1.

(b) 1.

2.

3.

4.

5.

(c) 1.

(d) 1. We-have helped to develop this into a beautiful and powerful thing.

2. During-the summer sales I-shall offer at cheap prices everything that-is left.

3. I-have helped to advertise this in every-way I could, and-this-is my final offer.

4. I-have measured-the table and-I-think it differs in size.

5. I-hope-you-can come sooner. Otherwise I-shall-not see-you because I-leave on-Friday.

LESSON TWENTY-SEVEN

REVERSE FORMS FOR FR, VR, THR

....⁀.... three, ...⌒.... weather, ..⌐ฺ.... free, ...⌐ฺ.. river,

..⤵.... before, ...ↄ....... Thursday, ...ฺ...... north, ...ↄฺ. engineer.

The double-consonants FR, VR, THR, and *THR* are provided with additional or " reverse " forms. The reverse forms are used in a one-syllable word which does not begin with a vowel; and generally when joined to a stroke written from left to right: .⁀... *through*, ⌐⌐ *cover*, ..⌐ฺ. *river.*

In a few words, in order to obtain short outlines, the hooked signs are used, even though a vowel other than E (as in *per*) comes before the R or L. A dot is expressed by writing a small circle in place of the dot; a dash or a diphthong is expressed by writing the sign through the double-consonant form: ...⤳...... *regard*, ...⌐₊ₚ.... *course.*

OUTLINE DRILL

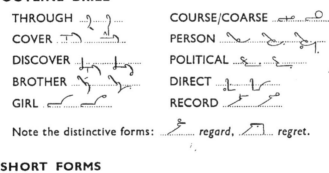

THROUGH ...⁀...⁀...   COURSE/COARSE ..⌐₊ₚ....⌐ₚ..

COVER .⌐⌐.......⌐⌐..   PERSON ..⤳......⤳......⤳...

DISCOVER ..⌊.......⌊..   POLITICAL ..⌐....,..⌐....

BROTHER ...⤳.....⤳....   DIRECT ..⌐...⌐...

GIRL .⌐........⌐....   RECORD ..⤳.......⤳....

Note the distinctive forms: ...⤳...... *regard*, ..⌐⌐.. *regret.*

SHORT FORMS

⌐⌐⌐⌐⌐⌐
.... character, ...⌐......... characters.

PHRASES

⤳ₚ
.... of course, ..⤳......... I regard the.

EXERCISE TWENTY-SEVEN

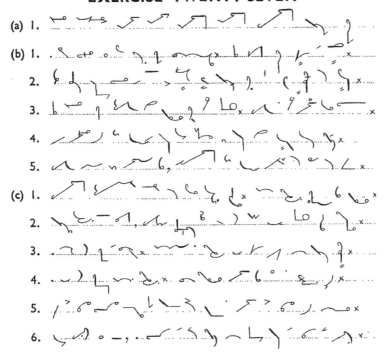

(d) 1. The personal efforts of-the engineer resulted in-the new road being put through.
2. I-believe you-will-have to-take different measures before you-can cover your losses.
3. The increase in sales is directly related to-the efforts of-the-employees.
4. The two brothers developed the engineering business themselves. They-have good personalities.
5. I-hope, of-course, to see-you before I-leave to-go north on-Thursday.
6. I-shall-be free at three. I-hope-the weather is good.

LESSON TWENTY-EIGHT

N HOOK—ADDED TO CURVES

_____ often, _____ than, _____ then, _____ lines.

A small hook at the end of a curve adds N. S Circle is added by writing the circle inside the Hook.

OUTLINE DRILL

EVEN _____ _____ _____

MINE _____ _____ _____

MAN _____ _____ _____

MEAN _____ _____ _____

MACHINE _____ _____

LINE _____ _____

KNOW _____ _____

SHOW _____ _____

SHORT FORMS

_____ from   _____ over   _____ within

_____ very   _____ however

PHRASES

_____ have been, _____ very much, _____ Very truly,

_____ Very truly yours, _____ Yours very truly.

Note the use of the N Hook to express the word *been*.

EXERCISE TWENTY-EIGHT

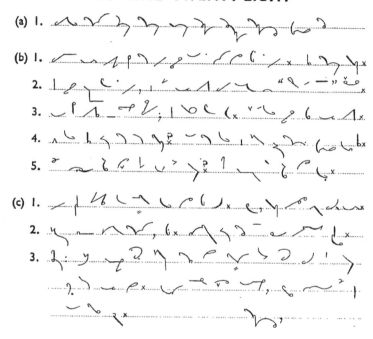

(a) 1.

(b) 1.

2.

3.

4.

5.

(c) 1.

2.

3.

(d) 1. Dear-Sir: It-is-not usual for-us to-make exchanges, but since you have-been a good customer of-ours, and-the machine you-are using is almost new, we-believe we-can make an offer for-it.

If-you-can bring-the machine to-our offices, we-shall-be-glad to-look it over. Otherwise our man can see it at your place within-the-next day or-two.

Yours-very truly,

LESSON TWENTY-NINE
N HOOK—ADDED TO STRAIGHT STROKES

⟍ upon, ⌡ down, ⌡ June, ⁀ again, ⌐ engine.

A small hook at the end of a straight stroke, written on the opposite side to S Circle, adds N.

OUTLINE DRILL

OPEN ⟍ ⟍

PLAN ⟋ ⟋

PLAIN/PLANE ⟍ ⟍

HAPPEN ⌒⟍ ⌒⟍

TRAIN ⌡ ⌐

BEGIN ⟍ ⟍ ⟍ ⟍

CLEAN ⌐ ⌐

ONE/WON ⟋ ⟍ ⟍

RUN ⟋ ⟋

TURN ⟍ ⟍

BURN ⟍

TOWN ⌡

CHILDREN ⟋

BETWEEN ⟋

LEARN ⌒

HUNDRED ⟍

JUNE ⌡

AGAIN ⁀

EXERCISE TWENTY-NINE

(a) 1.

(b) 1.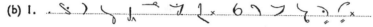

2.

3.

4.

5.

(c) 1.

2.

3.

4.

5.

6.

(d) 1. Dear-Sir: Within-the-next month or-two we-are planning to open one of-our stores in-your town. If-you happen to-have any knowledge of a good building that-is being advertised for sale, we should very-much like to-have details of-the price at-which it-is offered, and other details which-would-be helpful. Very-truly yours,

LESSON THIRTY

F OR V HOOK

.....⟍..... above, ...⟍.... gave, ...⟍.. half, ...⟍.... profit.

A small hook at the end of a straight stroke, written on the same side as S Circle, adds either F or V.

OUTLINE DRILL

CHIEF ....

DRIVE ....

PERFECT ....

PROFIT ....

PROVIDE ....

SERVE ....

There is no F or V hook to curves; the small hook at the end of a curve expresses N. Compare: .....⟍.. five, ...⟍.. fine; .....⟍.. knife, ...⟍.. nine; .....⟍.. move, ...⟍.. mean; .....⟍.. love, ...⟍.. line.

SHORT FORMS

.....|..... difficult   .....⟍..... been   ...../...... gentlemen

..|.......... difficulty   ...../...... general/generally   .... owe/oh

PHRASES

.....⟍...... has been, ... I gave, ...⟍..... it has not been.

EXERCISE THIRTY

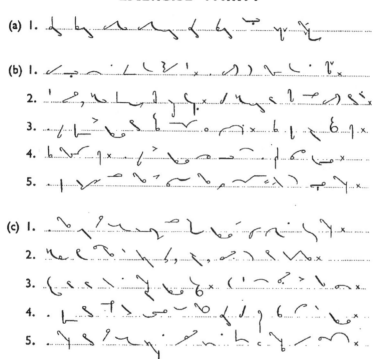

(d) 1. Gentlemen: The enclosed booklet shows the character of-our business, and suggests how we-can serve you and also how we-can increase your profits. Our business is-to help-you to-sell your goods, and our record has-been one of unbroken success. Our methods provide you with a means of-selling your products with less difficulty, and also enable-you to-cut your selling costs. If-you would like one of-our men to show you why and how we-can-be of service to-you, he-would-be happy to stop in for a personal talk. Yours-very-truly,

LESSON THIRTY-ONE

HALVING—FINALLY HOOKED STROKES

......⟋⟍...... pound, ...⟋...... second, ...⟋...... went, ...⟋....... learned.

A stroke that is hooked for N is halved to indicate a following T or D.

OUTLINE DRILL

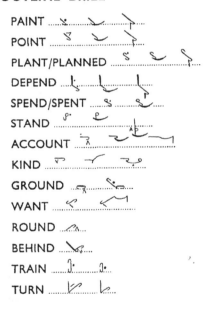

PAINT

POINT

PLANT/PLANNED

DEPEND

SPEND/SPENT

STAND

ACCOUNT

KIND

GROUND

WANT

ROUND

BEHIND

TRAIN

TURN

PHRASES

......⟋...... kind of, ...⟋...... on account of, ...⟋...... I went, ...⟋...... I want.

EXERCISE THIRTY-ONE

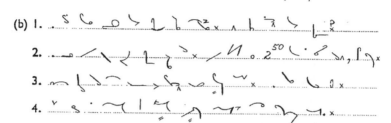

(d) 1. The plane left-the ground and-began its flight.

2. We-went for a drive to-the playground on-Thursday evening.

3. I-went to-the East River to-watch-the ship sail.

4. The city has opened a special playground behind-the bank.

5. Through-the kindness of-the buyer, I-have learned that-you have placed this on-the market.

6. The car turned round, and went over-the bank.

LESSON THIRTY-TWO

HALVING—FINALLY HOOKED STROKES, Continued

... ⌒ .. mind, ...ᔣ..... friend, ...➔... . gift, ...⌀?.... served.

A curve that is hooked for N is halved to indicate a following T or D. A stroke that is hooked for F or V is halved to indicate a following T or D.

OUTLINE DRILL

(a) AMOUNT ....ᔥ........ ⌒ ~

   DEMAND ....ᒷ.....ᒷ....ᒷ

   FIND ....ᔥ....ᔦ....~....ᔦ....

   EVENT ... ᔦ.......ᔦ....

   LAND ....ᒆ......ᒆ...

   FRONT ....ᔧ....ᔧ..

   MOMENT ...⌒ᔧ....⌒ᔦ..

   PAYMENT ....ᔦᔧ.........ᔦᔦ...

   SETTLEMENT ....ᒆ... ᒆ...

   STATEMENT ....ᒆ... ᒆ...

   DEVELOPMENT ..ᒪ......ᒪ....

(b) GIFT .....➔......⌀....

   SERVE ...⌀?....⌀?..

   HALVE ⌀?... ⌀?...

SHORT FORMS

....➔... cannot, ...(.. though, ...(. although.

PHRASES

....ᒍ.... do not, had not, ..ᒍ.. did not, ᒍ... had been, ...ᒇ.... out of.

Note the use of the N Hook to express *not* and *been*, and the use of the F Hook to express *of*.

EXERCISE THIRTY-TWO

(a) 1.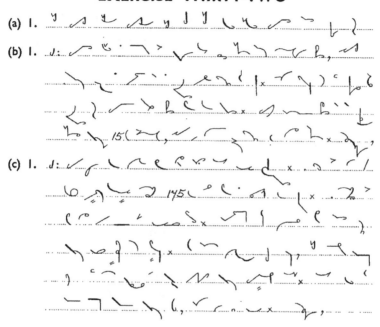

(b) 1.

(c) 1.

(d) 1. His friend said that my brother was out-of step with-the times.

2. His reason was that my brother had-not yet learned to fly.

3. Although our gifts are different from-the kind usually offered, . the prices are-not high.

4. Why not spend a few moments and look them over? Do you mind?

5. I-thought that-these payments had-been halved.

6. The check had-been returned because-the two amounts on-the face did-not agree.

7. Although his statement was-not very clear, it-has perhaps served its purpose.

LESSON THIRTY-THREE
CIRCLES AND LOOPS TO HOOKED STROKES

.......ᔑ....... strong, ...ᔑ᠆᠆... strange, ...�..... straight, ...🡒.... stopper,

....🖉°... once, ...⅘... spends, ...🡒......... against, ...🡓...... distances.

When a circle or loop comes before a *straight* double-consonant stroke of the .🡖.. per series, it is written on the R hook side of the sign. The circle or loop includes the R: ...413... str, ...🡒... skr.

When a circle or loop comes after N hook at the end of a *straight* sign, it is written on the N hook side of the stroke. The circle or loop includes the N: ..🡓.... tns, ..🡓... tnst, ..🡓.... tnstr.

OUTLINE DRILL

(a) STRANGE ....   DISTANT ....

STRONG ....   TRAIN ....

STRAIGHT ....   TOWN ....

STREET ....   ACCOUNT ....

STOPPER ....   DEPEND ....

(b) AGAIN ....   PLANT ....

ENGINE ....   POINT ....

CLEAN ....   GROUND ....

LEARN ....   WANT ....

DOWNWARD H BEFORE K, G

Downward H is used before K and G:

....🡓.... hook, ...🡒.... hog.

EXERCISE THIRTY-THREE

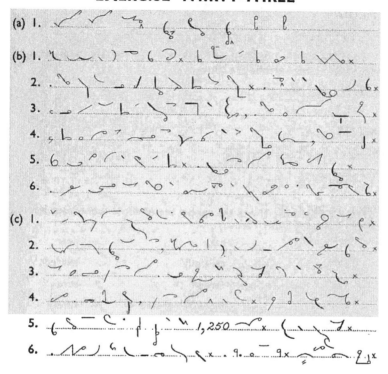

(d) 1. What-is-the distance between these two towns?

2. How often do-the trains run? Have-you any knowledge-of-the distance?

3. A strange thing happened to-him in-the street yesterday.

4. He wants us to-look at-these steel hooks as so-much depends upon them.

5. Some of-the plants have closed down, and-we-shall probably have difficulty in buying enough paper.

LESSON THIRTY-FOUR

MEDIAL S AND HOOKED STROKES

⟍ possible, ⟍ express, ⤵ industry.

In the middle of an outline, both the S Circle and the hook of a double-consonant stroke are shown.

OUTLINE DRILL

POSSIBLE

EXPRESS

INDUSTRY

DISTRIBUTE

SHORT FORMS. (Note the special use of double-consonant strokes in the following Short Forms.)

tell	care	near
told	carefully	neared
till	cared	sure
call	more/remark/ed	surely
called	remarkable/ly	short
gold	mere/Mr.	shortly
school	merely	shortage
balance	nor/in our	their/there
balanced		

PHRASES. (Note the use of the N hook to express *than*.)

there is, there are, to tell, they are, at all, by all, I am not, I will not, you are not, at once, more than, better than.

EXERCISE THIRTY-FOUR

(a) 1.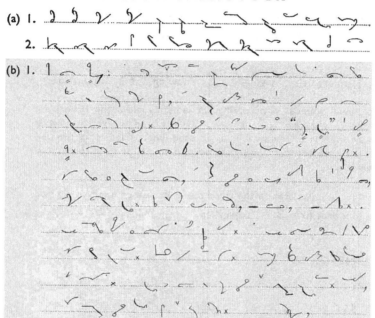

2.

(b) 1.

(c) 1. Though there-is-nothing difficult about-the job, you-must do it carefully.
2. If-you-are careless, you-will surely run into difficulties at-once.
3. We-have in-our list a book on-the care-of babies. Please balance the books.
4. We-are planning shortly to distribute copies as widely as possible.
5. They-have told-me very-little about-the remarkable new method they-are using.
6. I-am-not at-all sure of-their meaning. However, they-will-not tell-me.
7. The teacher at-once expressed her desire to see more of-the school, if at-all possible.
8. The chief industries of-the State are coal mining, and the manufacture of steel.

LESSON THIRTY-FIVE

DIPHONES

⌐⌐ happier, ⌐ saying, ⌐ knowing, ⌐ suggestion.

Two vowel sounds, one coming immediately after the other, are expressed by the sign ⌐ or ⌐ . ⌐ is used where the first of the two vowels is a dot vowel; ⌐ is used where the first of the two vowels is a dash vowel. The sign is written in the place of the first of the two vowels.

The sign ⌐ , written in the third place, is used to express the two vowels in words like ⌐ suggestion, ⌐ million.

OUTLINE DRILL

HAPPY	TRUE
HEAVY	IDEA
WEIGH	EXPERIENCE
SAY	SERIOUS
LOW	REALLY
SHOW	SUGGESTION
KNOW	MILLION
FOLLOW	

SHORT FORMS

owing/language   advantage   advantages

surprise   surprised   surprising

EXERCISE THIRTY-FIVE

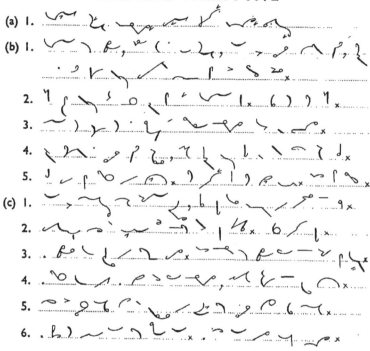

(d) 1. Within a short-time I-shall-be following your suggestion.

2. It-would-be to-your advantage to-take either of-these courses.

3. Make-up a statement showing-the advantages of-your suggestions.

4. We really think that-this-is a book which-will-be read by millions.

5. They-are weighing these-cases to see if they-are really heavier.

6. You-will-be happier, and truer to-yourself, if-you act upon this idea.

7. The enclosed statement shows the charges and payments during-the month and also shows the balance owing on-the last day of-the-month.

LESSON THIRTY-SIX

VOWEL INDICATION

⁀⌣ money, ⌢⌣ heavy, ⌇⌐ safety, ⌒⌐ window.

When a vowel sound follows F, V or N at the end of a word, a stroke F, V or N is written in order to place the sign. Compare: ⌒ men, ⌒⌢ many.

When a vowel sound follows T or D at the end of a word, the stroke T or D is written, in order to place the vowel sign. Compare: ⌇ bad, ⌇ body; ⌐ cost, ⌐ sixty.

OUTLINE DRILL

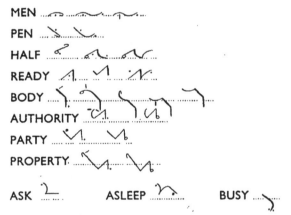

MEN

PEN

HALF

READY

BODY

AUTHORITY

PARTY

PROPERTY

ASK   ASLEEP   BUSY

The stroke S or Z is used at the beginning of an outline when a word begins with a vowel; and at the end of a word when there is a final vowel. Compare: ⌒ sack, ⌇ ask; ⌇ bees, ⌇ busy.

SHORT FORMS

/ large, ∮ largest, / larger, / largely, ⌇ whose.

EXERCISE THIRTY-SIX

(a) 1.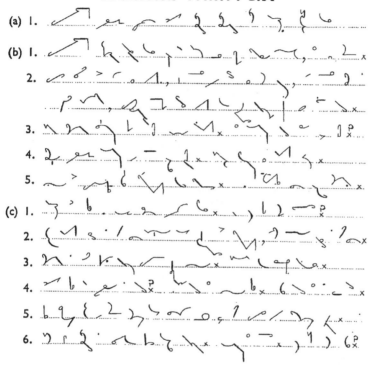

(b) 1.

2.

3.

4.

5.

(c) 1.

2.

3.

4.

5.

6.

(d) 1. This-is-the largest building on-the street and it-is called-the Newspaper Building.

2. Gold is-not now used for money; paper notes have-taken its place.

3. Keep all-the party in safety, and do-not let anybody go over to-the window.

4. I-have gone over-the statement carefully, and-I-believe that-their remarks are largely true.

5. I-have-been very busy, as I-want this property to-be ready for-the authorities soon.

LESSON THIRTY-SEVEN

CONSONANTS AR AND RAY

..:ᐯ.. early, ..ᐟ.. art, ⤝ᐟ. tomorrow, ..ᐟ.. country.

When a vowel comes before R at the beginning of a word, the downward *AR* is used.

When a vowel follows R at the end of a word, the upward *RAY* is used.

OUTLINE DRILL

(a) ART ..ᐟ.. ᐟ..   (b) CARRY ..⟋ ⟋ ⟋..

ARM ..ᐟᐟ ᐟ ᐟ..   MEMORY ..⌒⟋ ⌒⟋..

EARLY :ᐯ: ᐯᐟ ᐯᐟ..   STORY ᐟᐟ ᐟ ᐟ ᐟ..

IRON ..ᐟ ᐟ..   HISTORY ..ᐟᐟ ᐟᐟ..

ORDERED ᐟᐟ..

AROUND ᐟᐟ ⟋..

..⟋.. NECESSARY   ..⟋.. SUCCESS

..⟋.. NECESSITY   ..⟋.. SUCCESSFULLY

The large Circle is used to express S-S in the middle, as well as at the end, of a word.

SHORT FORMS

..⟋.. year, ..(.. thank/thanked, ..⟋.. opinion, ..⟋.. people,
..⟍.. public/publish/published, ..⟋.. regular, ..⟋.. regularly.

PHRASES

..⟍.. if it, ⟍.. if it is; ⟍.. care of, ..ᐟ.. who have.

Note the use of Halving to express the word *it* in a few phrases; and the use of the F or V Hook to express the word *have* in phrases.

EXERCISE THIRTY-SEVEN

(a) 1.

(b)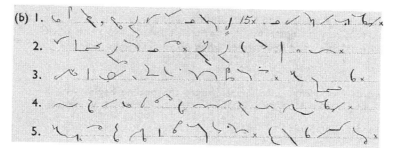

(c) 1.

    2.

    3.

    4.

    5.

    6.

(d) 1. Dear–Miss Black: Thank-you very-much for-your note. We-have-sent to-you today a sample copy of-our book " Stories About Our Country," which-we-have just published. In-our-opinion, this-is a book that really helps-the teacher of history. It-has-been specially written for children who-have-not-yet reached high-school age, and it relates in simple language many of-the outstanding events in-the history of-our country, from-its earliest days till-the present-time. We should like to-have-your opinion of-the book. Very-truly-yours,

LESSON THIRTY-EIGHT
UPWARD AND DOWNWARD L

....ʃ... full, ...ʃ... fully, ⌒ alike, ⌒ alone.

When L comes at the end of an outline and follows ＼... f, ＼... v,
◦— sk or a straight upstroke, it is written upwards when the word
ends with a vowel, and downwards when no vowel comes after the L.
Compare: ...ʃ... real, ...ʃ... really.

In words like *along, alike, alone*, where the outline begins with a
vowel and L is followed by a simple horizontal stroke, L is written
downwards. Compare: ⌒ *along*, ⌒ *long*.

OUTLINE DRILL

USEFUL

CAREFUL

SUCCESSFUL

FALL

FOLLOW

FEEL

RULE

RAIL

ALONG

ALIKE

PHRASES

.... with you, ... when you, ... what you, ...3.. would you.

EXERCISE THIRTY-EIGHT

(a) 1.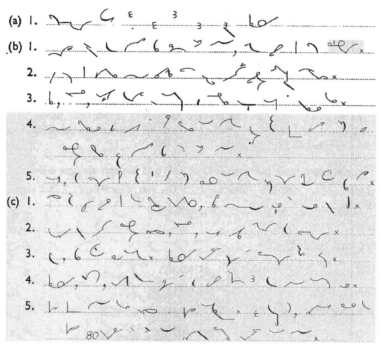

(b) 1.

   2.

   3.

   4.

   5.

(c) 1.

   2.

   3.

   4.

   5.

(d) 1. Since these signs are used so often, it-is very-much to-your advantage really to-master them.

   2. The best way to-learn them is to-copy them many-times, following-the examples carefully.

   3. The two brothers are alike in-that they-are both leading full, useful, and successful lives.

   4. You-will-not fall if-you hold-the rail and-follow these steps carefully.

   5. You-may go alone if-you-like, but it-would-be better to-take somebody along with-you.

LESSON THIRTY-NINE

HALVING FOR RT, RD: LT, LD

⟋⟍ expert, ⌒ heard, ⌄ built, ⌄ field, ⌒⌐ followed.

At the end of an outline, the upward form ⟋ is used to express RT. The downward form ⟍ (Downward AR halved and thickened) is used to express RD.

At the end of an outline, the upward form ⟋ is used to express LT; the downward form ⟍ (Downward L halved and thickened) is used to express LD.

If a vowel is sounded between R-D or L-D the full strokes are used. Compare: ⌄ sort, ⌒ hard; ⌄ felt, ⌄ field; ⟍ card, ⟍ carried; ⌄ fold, ⌒⌐ followed.

OUTLINE DRILL

PART ⌄ ⌄		HARD ⌒ ⌄	
START ⌐ ⌐		DESIRED ⌄	
SUPPORT ⌄ ⌄		CLEARED ⌐	
REPORT ⟋⌄ ⟋⌄		BOARD ⌄ ⌄	
FELT ⌄		OLD ⌄	
BUILT ⌄		CHILD ⌄	
MARRIED ⌒⌐		VALUED ⌒⌐	

PHRASES

⌒ sort of, ⌄ support of, ⌄ part of, ⌄ years ago, ⌒ last year, ⌄ I would.

EXERCISE THIRTY-NINE

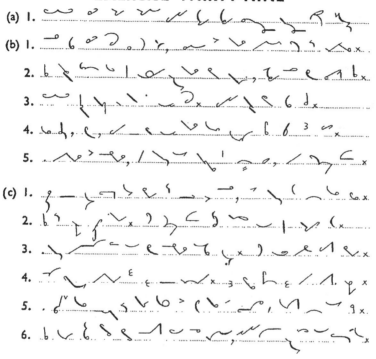

(a) 1.

(b) 1.

2.

3.

4.

5.

(c) 1.

2.

3.

4.

5.

6.

(d) 1. It-is hardly likely that old property of-this sort was bought for many hundreds of dollars above its real value.

2. The house was built many-years-ago, and such an old house would-not-be valued at-such a high figure.

3. Although we-have written several-times we-have-not-heard from-you.

4. I-would like to-hear more about your experiences on board the ship.

5. I-would-not support this sort-of plan, and I-could-not start on it.

LESSON FORTY

HALVING FOR ND, MD: FINAL -TED

..... send, ... thousand, ... made, ... modern.

Consonant stroke N is halved and thickened to indicate a following
D; consonant stroke M is halved and thickened to indicate a following
D. Compare: ..... neat, ... need; ..... meet, ... made.

OUTLINE DRILL

END ....

SOUND ....

NEED ....

MADE ....

MODERN ....

SIGN ....

SEEM ....

NAME ....

FINAL -TED. Following stroke ..... or ..... , -ted is expressed
by disjoined ..... , as: ..... dated, ... credited, ... doubted.

SHORT FORMS   SHORT FORM DERIVATIVES

..... hand   ..... immediate   ..... shorthand

..... under   ..... third   ..... longhand

..... yard   ..... particular   ..... understand

..... word   ..... opportunity   ..... understood

PHRASES

..... are you, ... can you, ... give you, ... send you, ... may not,
..... how are you, ... two-thirds, ... send us, ... for the words.

EXERCISE FORTY

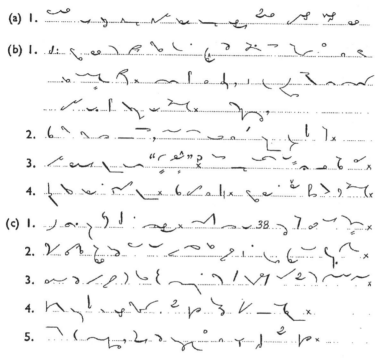

(d) 1. We-are-glad to-send-you-the booklets for-which-you ask.

2. If-you need more, we-can send them at-the-end of-the-month.

3. I-will-be on hand when-you need me. I-understood that-this was-the case. We-have credited your account, as-desired.

4. I-thought it-was understood that-you would distribute-the books at-the first opportunity.

5. A third was distributed in January, a third was sent out in February, and-we-expect to-send-the balance before-the end of-March.

LESSON FORTY-ONE

DOUBLING: Curves

.... matter, ... order, ... further, ... letter.

A curve is doubled in length to indicate that it is followed by the sound of TR, DR, *THR*, or TURE.

When L is the only stroke, it is doubled to add TR only. Compare:

.... *later*, ... *leader*.

NG is doubled to add the sound of KR or GR: .... *longer*.

OUTLINE DRILL

AFTER

MOTOR

MATTER

MATERIAL

ORDER

FATHER

ANOTHER

NEITHER

MOTHER

FUTURE

NATURE

LIGHT

LATE

LONG

SHORT FORMS

.... interest, ... interested, ... therefore.

EXERCISE FORTY-ONE

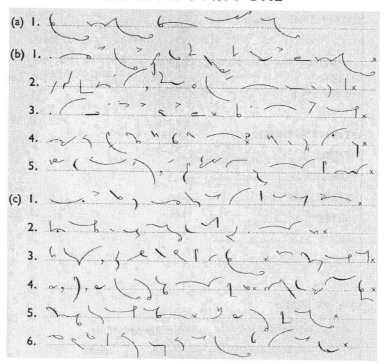

(d)
1. Neither of-the-men who signed-the letter had any interest in-the future of-the business.

2. Fire and-water are two of Nature's powerful forces.

3. I-shall motor into town to order another length of-this material.

4. I-may, therefore, be a little later than I-expected to-be.

5. He ordered that in-future all letters of interest must be passed to-him.

6. They-are making further tests before they order-the lighter weight material.

LESSON FORTY-TWO

DOUBLING: Straight Strokes

╲....... picture, ╲╱.... operator, ...╲... painter, ...|...... doubter.

A straight stroke is doubled to add the sound of TR, DR, THR, or TURE only when it follows another stroke or a circle, or when it has a final hook or a finally-joined diphthong.

OUTLINE DRILL

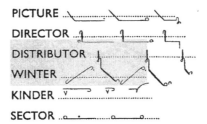

PICTURE ..╲................╲..........╲....,

DIRECTOR ..♩............♩............♩....

DISTRIBUTOR ..|............|............|....

WINTER ....╱......╲......╱......ₒₙ

KINDER ....ᵥ⎯⎯⁾......ᵥ⁾......⎯⎯

SECTOR ..ₒ....•..........ₒ..........ₒ......

SHORT FORMS

..╱....... rather/writer, ..╱....... wonderful/wonderfully,

..╲...... subject/subjected, ...ₓ...... speak, ...|...... itself.

PHRASES

....⌒.... as a matter of fact, ..╱..... rather than, ...ₓ....... to speak,

...⌐ₗ.... in itself, ...⌒.... in there/their, ...╿....... I think there is,

...╲....... I have been there.

In a phrase, the word *there* or *their* may be indicated by doubling.

EXERCISE FORTY-TWO

(a) 1.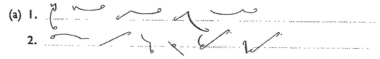

    2.

(b) 1.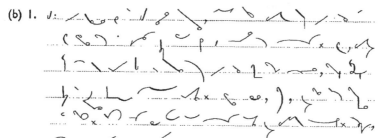

(c) 1.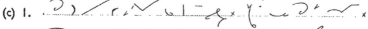

    2.

    3.

    4.

    5.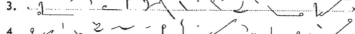

    6.

(d) 1. Teachers and writers have agreed that-it-is a subject in-which short-cuts do-not help.

    2. The writer in-his talk painted a wonderful picture of-the future.

    3. I-have-been-there in-the winter, and-have-had some wonderful times.

    4. As-a-matter-of-fact, it-would-be kinder to buy-the picture from-the painter.

    5. I-would rather leave-the writer to-speak for-himself on-this subject.

LESSON FORTY-THREE

PREFIX CON- (COM-)

 ⌇ control, ⌇ connect, ⌇ complete, ⌇ commit.

The prefix *con-* (or *com-*) is expressed by a dot placed at the beginning of the following stroke.

In the middle of a word the syllable *con-*, *com-*, *cog-*, or *cum-*, is indicated by disjoining, as:

⌇ *discontinue*, ⌇ *uncommon*, ⌇ *recognize*.

OUTLINE DRILL

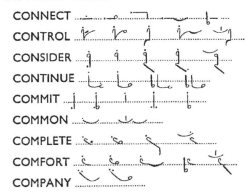

CONNECT

CONTROL

CONSIDER

CONTINUE

COMMIT

COMMON

COMPLETE

COMFORT

COMPANY

PHRASES

⌇ this committee, ⌇ are continuing, ⌇ that we consider.

Note that the syllable *con-* (or *com-*) is indicated in phrasing by writing the two outlines close together.

EXERCISE FORTY-THREE

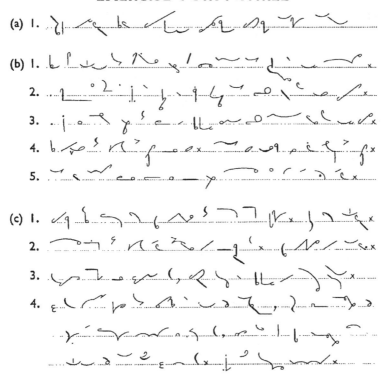

(a) 1.

(b) 1.

2.

3.

4.

5.

(c) 1.

2.

3.

4.

(d) 1. I-think-you-should-consider carefully taking another course rather-than-commit yourself to a step which-you might regret.

2. The company should discontinue-the uncontrolled sale of-these goods.

3. This-committee is seriously-considering making a complete change in-the-method of control.

LESSON FORTY-FOUR

SUFFIX -ING

 paying, ordering, mastering, serving.

The suffix -ing is generally expressed by . Where the use of the stroke is awkward, -ing is expressed by a dot placed at the end of an outline. The dot -ing is used: (a) After a light straight downstroke, or after downward R; (b) generally after a short form; and (c) in cases where the stroke form would not join conveniently. Where -ing is expressed by a dot, -ings is expressed by a dash: servings.

OUTLINE DRILL

PAYING

TRYING

TEACHING

REPLYING

HEARING

COVERING

COSTING

MEETING

MORNING

NON-USE OF HALVING

 minute, looked, fact, effect, rate, right/write, all right.

The halving principle is not used when the proper length of a halved stroke would not clearly show.

Half-length ray is not used unless it is joined to another stroke. Compare: operate, wrote.

SHORT FORM DERIVATIVES

 coming, interesting.

EXERCISE FORTY-FOUR

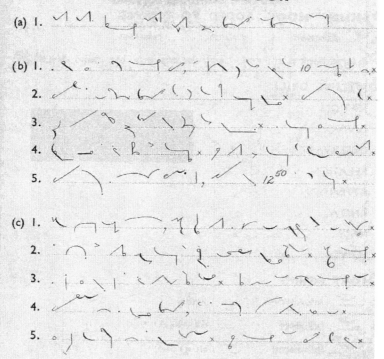

(a) 1.

(b) 1.

2.

3.

4.

5.

(c) 1.

2.

3.

4.

5.

(d) 1. Gentlemen: This-is-the third time this year that-we-have-had to-write to-you regarding your method of shipping our orders. Replying to-our last letter, you said that-you had-been meeting with considerable trouble in getting the right kind of-cases, but that-you had looked into-the matter, and-felt that-there-would-be no further difficulty. We-are-now writing to-you expressing surprise that-it-is-necessary for-us to-take up-the matter again. In-this-morning's delivery several cases had-been broken, and-we-are returning the goods immediately. Very-truly-yours,

LESSON FORTY-FIVE
"SHUN" HOOK—ADDED TO CURVES

attention,   division,   relations.

A large hook at the end of a stroke expresses the sound -SHUN.

OUTLINE DRILL

NATION

DIVISION

OBSERVATION

RELATION

ATTENTION

KNOW

MAY

LOW

SHORT FORMS

information

influence

influenced

own

owner

young

together

altogether

truth

principle
principal
principally

number/
numbered

member
remember
remembered

insurance

great

greater

PHRASES

number of, rate of, our own, young people, as to the, together with.

Note the use of the N hook to express the word *own* in phrases.

EXERCISE FORTY-FIVE

(c)
Hope, Pointing and-Company
Home Insurance Division
60 Market Street

Attention Mr.-Wright

Gentlemen: I-am-the owner of-the house at 52 River Avenue,
which-is covered by fire insurance that-you wrote last-year.
The insurance was issued at-the rate-of 45 cents a thousand,
costing me a total of $54 a year. I-understand, however, that-
the rates on-this-kind of-property are-now lower. If-this-is-
the case, when I-renew I should-be getting a larger-amount
of insurance at no greater cost. As-a-matter-of-fact, I-am
considering increasing-the amount since-the house is-now
valued at a considerably higher figure. I-would like, therefore,
full information as-to-the rates now in-effect. Thank-you for-
the attention you-will give this-matter. Yours-very-truly,

LESSON FORTY-SIX

"SHUN" HOOK—ADDED TO STRAIGHT STROKES

....✎.... station, ...✎.... completion, ...✎.... caution, ...✎.... competition.

When attached to a straight stroke, the SHUN Hook is written: (a) On the opposite side to an initial circle or hook; (b) on the opposite side to the last vowel if there is no initial circle or hook; (c) on the right side of T, D, or J.

SHUN following S or NS Circle is expressed by writing a small curved "tail" after the circle, as: ....✎.... *possession,* ....✎.... *taxation;* ....✎.... *transition.* A third place vowel between S and SHUN is placed outside this "tail" as: ....✎.... *positions.* Other vowels are not indicated.

OUTLINE DRILL

STATION ....✎....

CONSIDERATION ....✎.... ....✎....

CAUTION ....✎....

ACTION ....✎.... ....✎....

COMPLETION ....✎....

CONNECTION ....✎.... ....✎....

OPERATION ....✎.... ....✎.... ....✎....

EDUCATION ....✎.... ....✎....

PERFECTION ....✎....

DIRECTION ....✎.... ....✎....

DISTRIBUTION ....✎.... ....✎....

ADDITION ....✎.... ....✎.... ....✎.... ....✎.... ....✎....

CONDITION ....✎.... ....✎.... ....✎....

POSITION ....✎....

Note. The stroke SH and the N Hook are used to express *-uation.* Compare: ....✎.... *station,* ....✎.... *situation.*

PHRASES

....✎.... in addition, ...✎.... in connection with.

EXERCISE FORTY-SIX

(a) 1. [shorthand outlines]

(b) 1. [shorthand outlines]

2. [shorthand outlines]

3. [shorthand outlines]

4. [shorthand outlines]

(c) 1. [shorthand outlines]

2. [shorthand outlines]

3. [shorthand outlines]

4. [shorthand outlines]

5. [shorthand outlines]

(d) 1. Engineers have brought-the " air-conditioning " of homes and plants to a state-of perfection.

2. Please send to-the above address any-information you-may-have on-the subject.

3. Send it, together-with any additional information you-can supply regarding taxation.

4. The new station should soon be ready to-start operation.

5. Distribution of-the report should-be-made within a short-time to school directors and others interested in education.

LESSON FORTY-SEVEN

SEMI-CIRCLE FOR W; SWAY CIRCLE

weak/week, women, work, world.

When W begins a word, and is followed by _____ or _____, the sound is expressed by a small semi-circle.

To obtain a short outline, the semi-circle is sometimes used to express W in the middle of an outline: _____ quality, _____ frequent.

OUTLINE DRILL

WALK .... WORK ....

WAR .... WORTH ....

WARM .... QUALITY ....

WIRE .... QUALIFY ....

WERE .... FREQUENT ....

Note that the outline _____ *woman* is written above the line to distinguish it from _____ *women*.

SWAY CIRCLE

sweet, sweetly, sweetest, sweeter.

SW at the beginning of an outline is expressed by a large circle (called SWAY).

SHORT FORMS

income, become, whenever, whatever,

object/objected, objection.

PHRASES

as soon as, as well as, as we are, you were,

which were, we were, must be.

Note in the above phrases the special use of the large circle, the two forms for *were*, and the omission of *t* from *must*.

EXERCISE FORTY-SEVEN

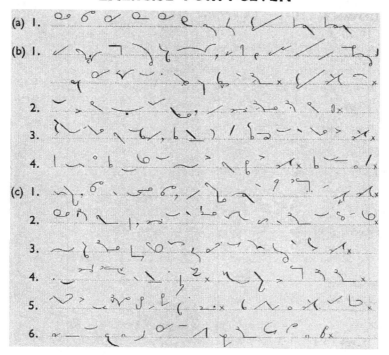

(d) 1. The order was shipped as-soon-as we-received your wire early last week.

2. We-think-there-is a considerable difference in-the quality of-the-goods which-were sent to-us.

3. The young woman has a sweet voice, but it-must-be trained.

4. Please ship to-us, as-soon-as you possibly can, a thousand feet of wire.

5. As-we-are within a mile of-the office, we frequently walk to work.

6. I-shall-have nothing whatever to-do with-this work as I-object to-the quality of-the material.

LESSON FORTY-EIGHT

DOWNWARD L; UPWARD SH

⌐ only, ⌐ until, ⌐ unless, ⌐ lessen, ⌐ senseless.

Stroke L following N or NG is written downward.

When L comes before or after a circle that is attached to a curve, it is written in the same direction as the circle. Compare: ↳ vessel, ╱ loosely.

OUTLINE DRILL

RECENT   HAND

CERTAIN   NEAR

STRONG   LESSEN

NATURAL   SENSE

INCREASING   MOST

Note the derivative forms: nearly, handle, additional.

UPWARD SH

fish, dish, official, fisher.

Stroke SH is sometimes written upwards to give a better outline.

SHL is always written upwards; SHR is always written downwards. Compare: fisher, official.

SHORT FORMS

pleasure, beyond, accord/according/according to, electric, electrical, electricity, English.

PHRASES

in accordance with, we have pleasure.

EXERCISE FORTY-EIGHT

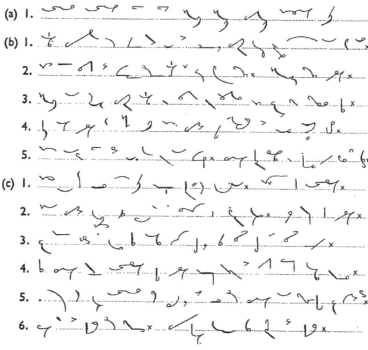

(d) 1. In a subject such-as this, an hour's regular work every-day is worth more-than many hours of effort once a week.

2. That-is why teachers are strongly of-the opinion that daily lessons are-the most effective.

3. Naturally, the more writing you do the sooner you-will-become an expert writer.

4. One expert recently told-me that not-only does he continually review-the rules, but that-it-is his custom to-copy-the notes in a book such-as this, line by line, always trying to-reach perfection in-the writing of-each outline.

LESSON FORTY-NINE

CONSONANTS AR AND RAY

.... warm, ... officer, ... wiser, ... disappear.

Downward R is always used before M.

Upward Ray is used: (a) after ....; (b) after a straight upstroke; (c) after two straight downstrokes.

Ray is used before the strokes ..|..|../../../.(..⌐..., as .... artist, ... arch, ... earth, ... article.

OUTLINE DRILL

ROOM ....

FARM ....

FORM ....

ANSWER ....

OFFICER ....

USER ....

WISER ....

CARRIER ....

DISAPPEAR .... but ....

DOWNSTAIRS ....

EARTH ....

STORE ....

SHORT FORMS

.... tried, ... trade/toward, ... equal/equally, ... equaled/cold, ... satisfactory, ... satisfactorily, ... represent/represented, ... respect/respected, ... inform/informed.

EXERCISE FORTY-NINE

(a) 1.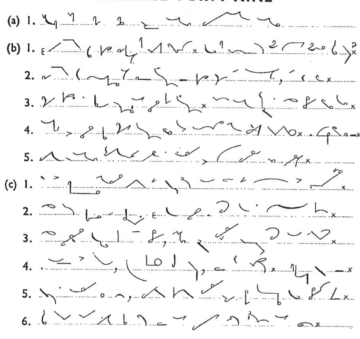

(b) 1.

2.

3.

4.

5.

(c) 1.

2.

3.

4.

5.

6.

(d) 1. I-think-that-the statement in-this respect is too weak and-I-have-tried to change it.

2. The purpose of-the plan was to provide a more equal distribution of-the natural products of-the earth to all-the people of-the world.

3. As trade between-the different nations grows, the national income increases.

4. We-are-informed that-their answer is-not altogether satisfactory.

5. The officer was wiser to disappear. He disappeared from-the farm during-the night.

LESSON FIFTY

COMPOUND CONSONANTS

Sign	Letter	Name	Examples	
C	QU	*kway*	quick,	quarter
C	GU	*gway*	Gwynn,	sanguine
⌒	MP/MB	*imp/imb*	camp,	December
C	LR	*ler*	fuller,	ruler
⌐	RR	*rer*	poorer,	clearer
⌐	WH	*whay*	where,	white
C	WL	*wel*	well,	willing
C	WHL	*whel*	while,	meanwhile

There are special signs for special combinations of sounds, as shown above. It should be noted: (a) that ⌒ may be doubled to add R, as: September; (b) when a vowel comes before C or C at the beginning of a word, the strokes ⌐ or ⌐ are used. Compare: while, awhile.

OUTLINE DRILL

QUESTION   WILL

REQUIRE   WHERE

QUICK   FULL

SHORT FORMS

⌒ important/importance, ⌒ impossible,
⌒ improve/improved/improvement, ⌐ whether,
⌐ organize/organized, ⌐ organization,
⌐ responsible/responsibility.

EXERCISE FIFTY

(a) 1.

(b) 1.

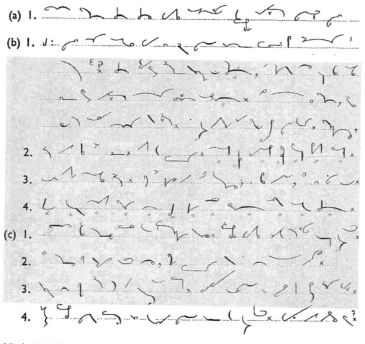

2.

3.

4.

(c) 1.

2.

3.

4.

(d) 1. While I-am willing to-believe that-this new system is an improve-
       ment and-will result in improved service, I-think-we should
       wait awhile before changing over to-it.

   2. The undertaking is a big responsibility. We-have-not-yet had
      an opportunity to-tell whether-the new methods are likely
      to-be satisfactory to-our organization.

   3. Meanwhile, although our present system is not altogether satis-
      factory, it-will meet most of-our requirements.

   4. You-are-now well on-your way towards mastering the subject
      of-shorthand writing.

APPENDIX ONE
TABLE OF CONSONANTS

Sign	Letter	Name	As in			
＼	P	*pee*	paid	up		
＼	B	*bee*	body	back		
⫯	T	*tee*	take	touch		
⫯	D	*dee*	deep	followed		
／	CH	*chay*	cheap	touch		
／	J	*jay*	judge	age		
—	K	*kay*	keep	came		
—	G	*gay*	got	big		
⌒	M	*em*	make	came		
⌒	N	*en*	change	know		
⌒	NG	*ing*	changing	being		
⌒	F	*eff*	food	safe		
⌒	V	*vee*	view	save		
(	TH	*ith*	both	think		
(	TH	*thee*	they	them		
)	S	*ess*	so	see		case
)	Z	*zee*	ease	was		views
⌐	SH	*ish*	show	shall		
⌐	ZH	*zhee*	usual/ly	measure		
⌐ (Down)	R	*ar*	arm	fear		
⟋ (Up)	R	*ray*	rate	carry		
⌒ (Up)	L	*el*	long	fully		
⌒ (Down)	L	*el*	along	full		
⟋	W	*way*	weigh	wide		
⟋	Y	*yay*	yes	use		
⟋ (Up)	H	*hay*	happy	head		
⟍ (Down)	H	*hay*	high	he		
／ (Dash or Tick)	H	*hay*	home	hold		here

VOWEL REVIEW

1. There are twelve vowel signs in Pitman Shorthand and three places in which these vowel signs may be put, the first, second, and third places.

(a) The first place vowels are—

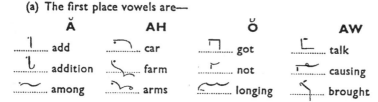

Ă	AH	Ŏ	AW
add	car	got	talk
addition	farm	not	causing
among	arms	longing	brought

When the first vowel sound in a word is a first-place vowel the outline is written above the line.

(b) The second place vowels are—

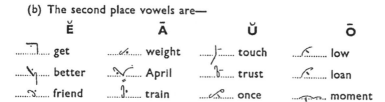

Ĕ	Ā	Ŭ	Ō
get	weight	touch	low
better	April	trust	loan
friend	train	once	moment

If the first vowel sound is a second-place vowel the outline is written on the line.

(c) The third place vowels are—

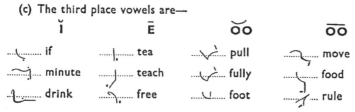

Ĭ	Ē	ŎŎ	ŌŌ
if	tea	pull	move
minute	teach	fully	food
drink	free	foot	rule

When the first vowel sound in a word is a third place vowel the outline is generally written through the line. Such outlines are, however, written on the line: (1) When all the strokes in the outline are

horizontal signs, as: .... key, ... king; (2) When the first upstroke
or downstroke is half length, e.g. .... foot, ... football, ... wit,
.... witness, ... military.

2. There are four diphthong signs in Pitman Shorthand, two written
in the first place and two in the third place.

(a) The first place diphthongs are—

Ī	OI	as in the outlines
.... buy	.... boy	
.... like	.... voice	
.... drive	.... joy	
.... isle	.... oil	

(b) The third place diphthongs are—

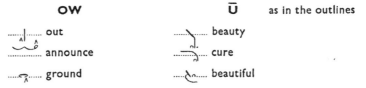

OW	Ū	as in the outlines
.... out	.... beauty	
.... announce	.... cure	
.... ground	.... beautiful	

The diphthong signs for OW and Ū are joined at the end of a downstroke—

.... doubt	.... few
.... bough	.... feud
.... powder	.... due

The sign for Ū may be turned on its side to obtain a good joining:
 .... new, ... value.

3. A vowel sound that follows a diphthong sound is expressed by adding a small dash to the diphthong sign. The sign thus formed is called a TRIPHONE. For example—

Ī   plus vowel: ......\...... buyer, ...\...... via

OI   plus vowel: ......)...... boyish, ...\...... employer

OW   plus vowel: ......\...... power, ...\...... towel

Ū   plus vowel: ......\...... fewer, ...\...... newer

4. When two vowels come together but are each sounded separately the small signs ...ᴄ.... and ...ᴀ.... are used. These signs are called DIPHONES.

The sign ...ᴄ.... is used when the first of the two vowels is a dot vowel and it is put in the place of the first of the two vowels: ...ᴨ... real, ...ᴨ..... really, ... material, ...ᴠ.... experiences, ...ᴄ..... layer.

The sign ...ᴀ..... is used when the first of the two vowels is a dash vowel, and it is put in the place of the first of the two vowels: ...ᴀ.... lower, ...ᴀ.... lowest, ... knowing, ... following, ...ᴧ.... truer, ...ᴧ.. jewel.

5. In outlines using the hooked forms \ \ \ \, etc., it is sometimes desired to show that a vowel other than ĕ (the vowel in per) comes between the first consonant and the R or L. The vowel may be indicated by—

(a) Writing a small circle in the place of a dot vowel: ...ᴄ.... regard, ... garment, ...ᴠ.... parcel, ...ᴧ.... direct, ...ᴧ.... engineer.

(b) Writing a dash vowel or a diphthong sign through the hooked form: .... north, ...ᴄᴛᴘ. course, ...ᴧ..., Thursday, ...\ᴠ. before, ...ᴄ...ᴧ.. lecture.

TABLE OF VOWEL AND DIPHTHONG SIGNS

Place	Vowels Short	Long	Diphthongs	Triphones	Diphones	Hooked form Vowels and Diphthongs
1st	add	car	like	buyer	naive	barometer · regard
2nd	get	train	out	towel	layer · real	questionnaire · direct · engineer
3rd	if	tea				
1st	got	talk	boy	employer	sawing	north · Thursday
2nd	trust	low			lower	before
3rd	book	food	duty	newer	truer	fulfill · lecture

1. Vowels and Diphthongs to Circle SeZ* exhaust, exist, insist, Mississippi, exercise, crisis, Kansas, basis, cases, passes.

2. Vowels to SHUN and S-SHUN addition, vision, conclusion, delusion, education, position, musician.

* When a vowel other than short ĕ occurs between the two consonants, it is indicated by placing the vowel sign inside the circle.

TABLE OF CIRCLES AND LOOPS

Initial

S CIRCLE					
SWAY CIRCLE					
STEE LOOP					

Final

S CIRCLE					
SEZ CIRCLE					
STEE and STER LOOPS					

Medial

| CIRCLES and LOOPS | | | | | |

TABLE OF OUTLINES USING STROKES S AND Z

1. ⌒ saw, ⌒ us, ⌒ ease, ⌒ easily, ⌒ sawdust.

2. ⌒ science, ⌒ scientific, ⌒ suet.

3. ⌒ size, ⌒ sizes, ⌒ saucer, ⌒ season, ⌒ society.

4. ⌒ continuous, ⌒ joyous, ⌒ pious.

5. ⌒ possess, ⌒ access, ⌒ excess.

6. ⌒ zeal, ⌒ zealous, ⌒ zealously.

NOTES.

The STROKE S is used:

1. In outlines derived from a " root " form using stroke S.

2. In outlines where a triphone immediately follows initial S.

3. In outlines where initial S is followed by a vowel and another S or Z.

4. In outlines for words where the final syllable -ous is preceded by a diphthong.

5. In a few outlines ending with S-S, to distinguish them from outlines in which the SEZ Circle is used.

Compare: ⌒ access, ⌒ axis; ⌒ possess, ⌒ poses.

The STROKE Z is used:

6. When Consonant Z begins a word.

108

TABLE OF HOOKED SIGNS

HOOKS ADDED TO STRAIGHT SIGNS

R

L

N

F/V

HOOKS ADDED TO CURVES

R

L

LEFT AND RIGHT FORMS FOR FR, FL, etc.

* R Hook is added to stroke ⌣ to express the sound *ng-kr* or *ng-gr*.

† After — — ⌒ or a straight upstroke, the right or " reverse " forms ((are used.

TABLE OF HOOKED SIGNS (Contd.)

N ADDED TO
CURVES

SHUN

S CIRCLE INSIDE
HOOK

S CIRCLE COMBINED
WITH HOOK

VOWELS TO HOOKED
FORMS

* Note such outlines as: ...... disagree, ... discourage.

110

TABLE OF PREFIXES

There are some syllables which occur very frequently at the beginning of a word. Special shorthand signs are used for such Prefixes, as follows—

CON-, COM-   Expressed by a dot, as:
                 ...condition, ...complete, ...company.

CON-, COM-,   When the syllable CON-, COM-, CUM-, or COG-
CUM-, COG-   comes in the middle of an outline or phrase it is
                 expressed by writing two strokes close to each other,
                 as: ...recognize, ...recommendation,
                 ...circumference, ...I will consider.

SELF-   Expressed by a disjoined S Circle, as:
                 ...self-defence, ...self-made.

SELF-CON-   Expressed by an S Circle, written in the place of
                 the CON- Dot, as: ...self-control.

IN-   Before ...Expressed by a small hook,
                 as: ...instruct, ...inscriber, ...inhabit.
                 Note the Short Forms:
                 ...instruction, ...instructions.

ACCOM-   Expressed by K, joined or disjoined, as:
                 ...accomplish, ...accompany,
                 ...accommodate.

INTRO-   Expressed by ...as: ...introduce,
                 ...introspection.
                 Short Form: ...introduction.

MAGNA-, I-, E-   Expressed by a disjoined M, as:
                 ...magnetize, ...magnificent.

TRANS-   Expressed by ...(omitting N), as:
                 ...transmission, ...transfer, ...transport.

TABLE OF SUFFIXES

There are some syllables which occur very frequently at the end of a word. Special shorthand signs are used for such Suffixes as follows:

-ING Often expressed by stroke . A small dot is used, however:

(a) After a light downstroke or downward R, as: paying, teaching, hearing.

(b) After a hook, circle, or loop where the stroke could not easily be joined, as: morning, serving, costing.

(c) Generally after Short Forms, as: thinking, coming.

Note the use of the stroke in having, doing, going, being.

-INGS Expressed by a light dash in cases where -ING would be expressed by a dot, as: mornings, servings, costings.

-MENT Expressed by when the hooked form would not be convenient, as: announcement, pavement.

Short Form: Government.

-MENTAL/LY Expressed by disjoined as: fundamental, temperamental.

-FULNESS Expressed by disjoined , as: carefulness, hopefulness.

-LESSNESS   Expressed by disjoined ⌒, as:
carelessness, hopelessness.

-SHIP   Expressed by joined or disjoined ⌿, as:
hardship, friendship, membership.

-LITY, -RITY   Expressed by disjoining the consonant stroke coming before, as:
possibility, formality,
majority, regularity.

-LOGICAL/LY   Expressed by disjoined J, as:
biological/ly, geological/ly.

-WARD   Expressed by ⌿, as:
forward, forwarding,
backward, afterwards.
Note forwarded.

-YARD   Expressed by ⌿, as:
backyard, shipyards.

-LY   Expressed (1) By Stroke L, joined or disjoined, as:
clearly, friendly, particularly.

(2) By the use of a hooked form, as:
cheaply, deeply, beautifully.

INTERSECTIONS

Certain words are so common that they may be represented in shorthand by a stroke written: (a) through a preceding or following outline; or (b) close to a preceding outline, as follows:

Sign	Word	As in
＼	PARTY	╳ our party
		╳ government party
＼	BANK	this bank
		reserve bank
	ATTENTION	special attention
		early attention
/	CHARGE	heavy charge
		free of charge
—	COMPANY	your company
		new company
—	GOVERNMENT	this government
		present government
⌣	FORM	new form
		necessary form
(	MONTH	this month
		for a month
⌢	MORNING	Saturday morning
		this morning
⌢	NATIONAL	national situation
		national business

Sign	Word	As in
⟋	REQUIRE	you may require
⟋	REQUIRED	will be required
⟋	REQUIREMENT	to meet requirements
⟋	RAILROAD or	railroad officials
	RAILWAY	railway company
⟍	ARRANGE	I will arrange
⟍	ARRANGED	they arranged
⟍	ARRANGEMENT	this arrangement
		these arrangements
⟍	SOCIETY	dramatic society
		medical society
⟍	BILL	education bill
⎮	DEPARTMENT	insurance department
⟋	JOURNAL	school journal
—	CAPTAIN	Captain Baker
⟱	COLONEL	Colonel Baker
⟱	CORPORATION	investment corporation
⟍	PROFESSOR	Professor Smith

· FIGURES

The signs ⟍⟍(⟍ are used for HUNDRED, THOUSAND, MILLION, as:

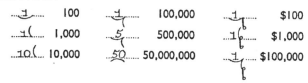

1	100	1	100,000	1	$100
1(	1,000	5	500,000	1(	$1,000
10(	10,000	50	50,000,000	1	$100,000

LIST OF THE 700 COMMON
SHORTHAND OUTLINES

(Representing approximately 68 per cent of ordinary English matter)

a/an	also	attention
able	altogether	August
about	am	authority
above	among	away
according	amount	baby
account	and	back
across	animal	bad
act	announce	balance
add	another	bank
advantage	answer	base
advertise advertised advertisement	any/in	be
after	appear	beautiful
afternoon	April	because
again	are	become
age	arm	bed
ago	army	before
agree	art	begin
air	as/has	behind
all	ask	belief believe believed
along	at	best
	attempt	

better

between

beyond

big

black

blue

board

body

book

both

bought

boy

brake (see break)

bread

break/brake

bring

brother

brought

build/building

built

burn

business

but

buy/by

call

came

can

capital

car

care

carry

case

cause

cent

certain

change

character

charge

cheap

check

chief

child

children

city

clean

clear

coal

coarse (see course)

cold

color

come

comfort

commit

common

company

competition

complete

condition

connect

consider

continue

control

copy

cost

could

country

course/coarse

cover

credit

cry

custom

cut

danger

date

day

dear

December

deep

degree

deliver
delivered
delivery

demand

depend

desire

detail

develop

die

differ

difference
different

difficult

difficulty

direct

discover

distance

distribute

distribution

division

dollar

do

door

doubt

down

dress

drink

drive

during

each

early

earth

ease

east

education

effect

either

electric

electricity

employ

end

engine

engineer

English

enough

equal/equally

even

event

ever

every

example

except

exchange
exchanged

exist

expect
expected

experience

expert

express

eye (see I)

face

fact

fall

family

far

farm

father

fear	front	happy
February	full	hard
feel	fully	has (see as)
few	further	have
field	future	he
figure	gave	head
final	general / generally	health
find	gentlemen	hear/here
fire	get	heart
first	girl	heat
fish	give/given	heavy
fly	go	help
follow	gold	her
food	good	here (see hear)
foot	govern / governed	high
for	government	him
force	great	himself
form	ground	his (see is)
forward	grow	history
free	had	hold
frequent	half	hole (see whole)
Friday	hand	home
friend	happen	hope
from		hour (see our)

house	is/his	leave
how	issue	left
however	it	less
hundred	itself	let
I/eye	January	letter
idea	judge	life
if	July	light
immediate	June	like
important importance	just	limit
	keep	line
impossible	kind	list
improve improved improvement	knew (see new)	little
in (see any)	know (see no)	live
increase	knowledge	long
indeed	labor	longer
industry	land	look
influence	language/owing	loss
inform informed	large	love
information	last	low
instruction	late	machine
insurance	law	made
interest	lead	make
iron	learn	man
	least	manufacture manufactured

many	minute	need
March	miss	neither
mark	modern	never / November
market	moment	new/knew
marry	Monday	news
mass	money	next
master	month	night
matter	more	no/know
may	remark / remarked	nor
me	morning	north
meal	most	not
mean	mother	note
measure	motor	nothing
meat/meet	move	November (see never)
member (see remember)	Mr. (see mere)	now
memory	much	number / numbered
mere/Mr.	must	object / objected
method	my	observation
might	myself	October
mile	name	of
milk	nation	off
million	nature	offer
mind	near	
mine	necessary	

office	owe (see Oh!)	plane (see plain)
official	owing (see language)	plant
often		play
Oh!/owe	own	please
oil	page	pleasure
old	paint	point
on	paper	political
once	part	poor
one	particular	position
only	party	possible
open	pass	pound
operate	pay	power
opinion	peace/piece	present
opportunity	penny	price
or	people	principal principally principle
order	perfect	
organize organized	perhaps	probable probably probability
organization	person	
other	personal	product
ought	picture	profit
our/hour	piece (see peace)	property
ourselves	place	provide
out	plain/plane	public publish published
over	plan	

pull	remark remarked (see more)	same
purpose		satisfactory
put	remember remembered member	Saturday
quality		save
quarter	report	say
question	represent represented	school
quick		sea (see see)
quite	require	second
railroad	respect respected	see/sea
rate	responsible responsibility	seem
rather/writer		seen
reach	rest	self
read	result	sell
ready	return	send
real	right/write	sense
really	river	sent
reason	road	September
receive	room	serious
recent	round	serve
record	rule	service
red	run	set
regard	safe	several
regular	said	shall
relate	sail/sale	she

ship	stand	surprise
short	start	sweet
should	state	system
show	station	table
side	steel/steal	take
sign	step	talk
simple	still	tax
since	stone	teach
sir	stop	tell
sit	store	test
situation	story	than
six	straight	thank/thanked
size	strange	that
small	street	the
so	strong	their/there
some	subject subjected	them
sometimes	success	themselves
soon	such	then
sort	suggest	there (see their)
sound	summer	therefore
south	Sunday	these
speak	supply	they
special specially	support	thing
spend/spent	sure	think

...)..... third

.....(..... this

.....(..... those

.....(..... though

.....(..... thought

...(..... thousand

....)..... through

....?..... Thursday

....f..... till

....L..... time

......\..... to

....L..... together

.....f..... told

....~..... tomorrow

....\..... too/two

.....)..... touch

......1..... toward/trade

.....f..... town

trade (see toward)

....)..... train

....?..... tried

....?..... trouble

....?..... true

....L..... trust

.....?.... truth

.....?.... try

.....f.... Tuesday

...V.... turn

two (see too)

....~..... under

....Y.... until

....λ.... up

....λ.... upon

....-).... us

....?.... use

....J.... usual/usually

....υ.... value

....η.... very

....L.... view

....υ.... voice

....μ.... wait/weight

....υ.... walk

....υ.... want

....λ.... war

....~.... warm

....).... was

....ε.... waste

....λ.... watch

.....λ..... water

....ε..... way/weigh

....ε..... we

weak (see week)

....ε..... weather

....~..... Wednesday

...~..... week/weak

weigh (see way)

weight (see wait)

....6..... well

....υ..... went

....λ..... were

....ε..... west

....)..... what

....ζ..... whatever

......ε...... when

....ς....... whenever

....ε..... where

....ε..... whether

....∕..... which

....ζ..... while

....υ..... white

....∕..... who

whole/hole		within		writer (see rather)	
whom		without		writing	
whose		woman		written	
why		women		wrong	
wide		wonderful wonderfully		yard	
will		word		year	
window		work		yes	
winter		world		yesterday	
wire		worth		yet	
wise		would		you	
wish		write (see right)		young	
with				your	

REVIEW CHART OF SHORT FORMS WITH RELATED
OUTLINES AND ADDITIONAL CONTRACTIONS

REVIEW CHART OF SHORT FORMS
WITH RELATED OUTLINES

A, an
  according
    advantage
advantageous
  advertise/d/ment
    all
altogether
  and
    any
anything
  are
    as
balance
  balanced
    be
become
  because
    been
belief
  believe/d
    beyond
build/ing
  but
    call
called
  can
    cannot
care
  cared
    character
characteristic
  cold
    come
could
  danger
    dangerous
dear
  deliver/ed/y
    difference/ent

difficult
  difficulty
    do
dollar
  during
    electric
electrical
  electricity
    English
equal/ly
  everything
    exchange/d
expect/ed
  eye
    February
first
  for
    from
general/ly
  generalization
    gentleman
gentlemen
  give/n
    go
gold
  govern/ed
    government
great
  had
    hand
handle
  has
    have
he
  him
    himself
his
  hour
    how

however
I
  immediate
important/ce
  impossible
    improve/d/ment
in
  income
    influence
influenced
  influential/ly
    inform/ed
information
  informer
    instruction
instructive
  insurance
    interest
is
  it
    itself
January
  knowledge
    language
large
  larger
    largely
manufacture/d
  manufacturer
    me
member
  mere
    more
most
  Mr.
    much
myself
  near
    never

REVIEW CHART OF SHORT FORMS
WITH RELATED OUTLINES

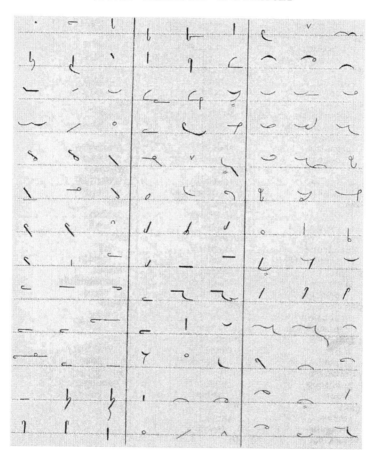

next
  nor
    nothing
November
  number/ed
    object/ed
objection
  objectionable
    objective
of
  Oh!
    on
opinion
  opportunity
    organization
organize/d
  organizer
    ought
our
  ourselves
    over
owe
  owing
    own
owner
  particular
    particularly
people
  pleasure
    principal/ly
principle
  probable/y/ility
    production
productive
  public
    publish/ed
publication
  publisher
    put
quite
  rather
    regular
remark/ed
  remarkable/y
    remember/ed

represent/ed
  representative
    representation
respect/ed
  respectful
    respectfully
respective
  respectively
    responsible/ility
satisfactory
  school
    schooled
sent
  several
    shall
short
  should
    something
speak
  special/ly
    subject/ed
subjection
  subjective
    sure
surprise
  surprised
    tell
thank/ed
  thankful
    that
the
  their
    them
themselves
  there
    therefore
thing
  think
    third
this
  those
    though
till
  to
    to be

together
  told
    too
toward
  towards
    trade
tried
  truth
    two
under
  usual/ly
    very
was
  we
    welcome
what
  whatever
    when
whenever
  whether
    which
who
  whose
    why
wish
  with
    within
without
  wonderful/ly
    word
would
  writer
    yard
year
  yesterday
    you
young
  younger
    youngest
your

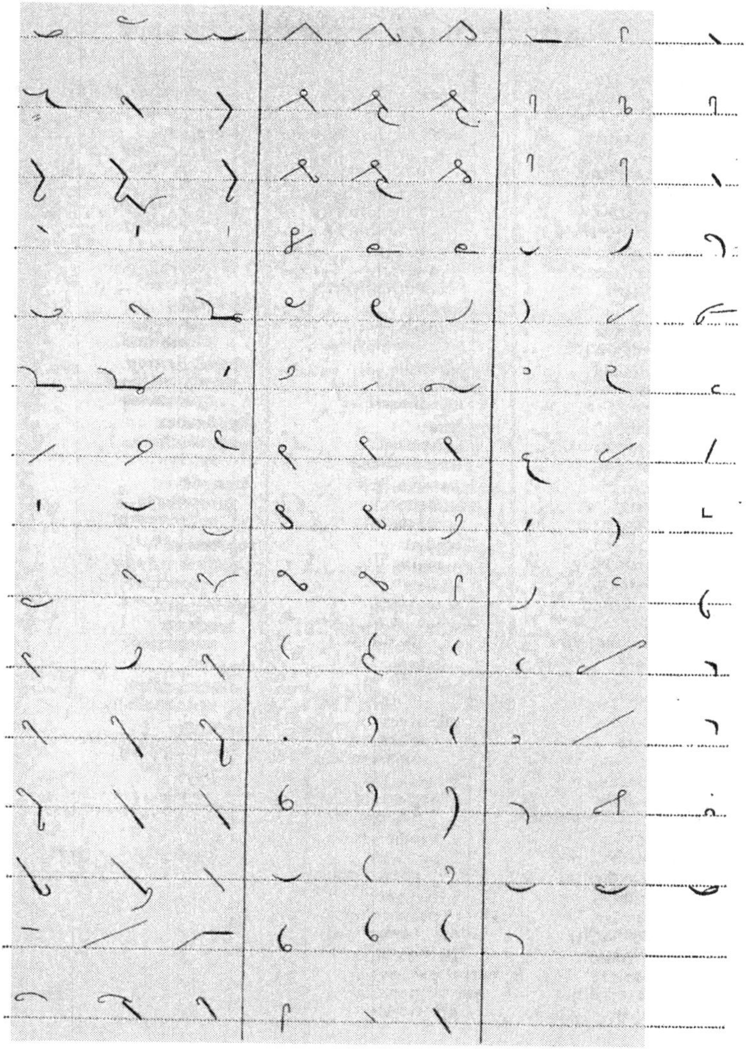

ADDITIONAL CONTRACTIONS

acknowledge
  acknowledgment
    administration
administrative
  administrator
    appointment
arbitrary
  arbitration
    architect/ure/al
assignment
  bankruptcy
    behalf
capable
  certificate
    circumstance
commercial/ly
  contentment
    defective
deficient/ly/cy
  democracy/atic
    demonstrate
demonstration
  description
    destruction
destructive
  destructively
    discharge/d
distinguish/ed
  doctor
    efficient/ly/cy
emergency
  England
    enlarge
enlargement
  enlarger
    entertainment
enthusiastic/m
  especial/ly
    establish/ed/ment
executive
  executor
    expediency
expenditure
  expensive
    familiar/ity
familiarization
  familiarize
    financial/ly

guard
  identical
    identification
imperfect/ion/ly
  inconvenient/ly/ce
    incorporated
independent/ly/ce
  indispensable/ly
    individual/ly
inscribe/d
  inscription
    inspect/ed/ion
intelligence
  intelligent/ly
    intelligible/y
introduction
  investigation
    investment
irregular
  irrespective
    irrespectively
irresponsible/ity
  jurisdiction
    justification
legislative
  legislature
    liberty
manuscript
  mathematics
    maximum
mechanical/ly
  messenger
    minimum
ministry
  misfortune
    monstrous
mortgage/d
  neglect/ed
    negligence
nevertheless
  northern
    notwithstanding
passenger
  peculiar/ity
    perform/ed
performance
  performer
    practicable

practice/se/d
  prejudice/d/ial/ly
    preliminary
project/ed
  proportion/ed
    prospect
prospective
  questionable/ly
    reform/ed
reformer
  reproduction
    republic
republican
  satisfaction
    selfish/ness
sensible/ly/ility
  signify/ied/icant
    significance
signification
  southern
    spirit
stranger
  subscribe/d
    subscription
substantial/ly
  sufficient/ly/cy
    suspect/ed
sympathetic
  telegram
    telegraphic
thus
  transcription
    unanimous/ly
unanimity
  uniform/ity/ly
    universal
universality
  universe
    university
unprincipled
  valuation

ADDITIONAL CONTRACTIONS

ADDITIONAL LETTERS FOR
READING AND DICTATION PRACTICE

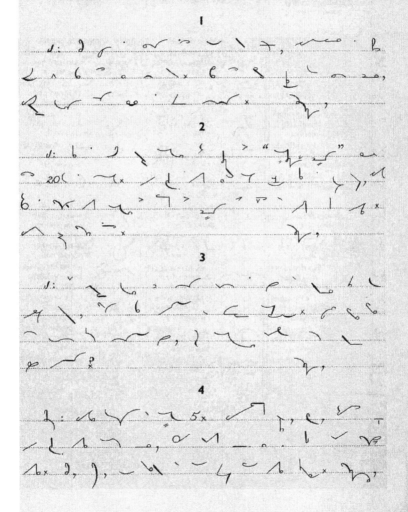

5

6

7

8

9

10

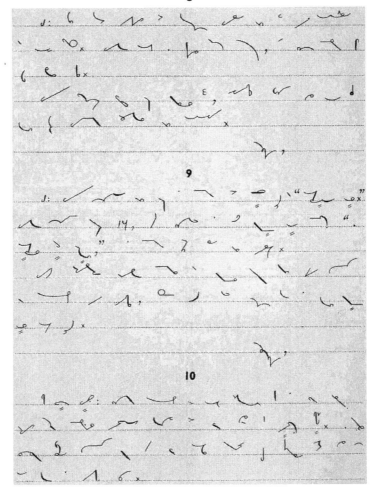

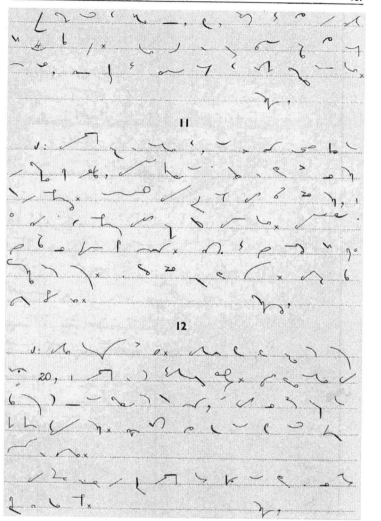

13

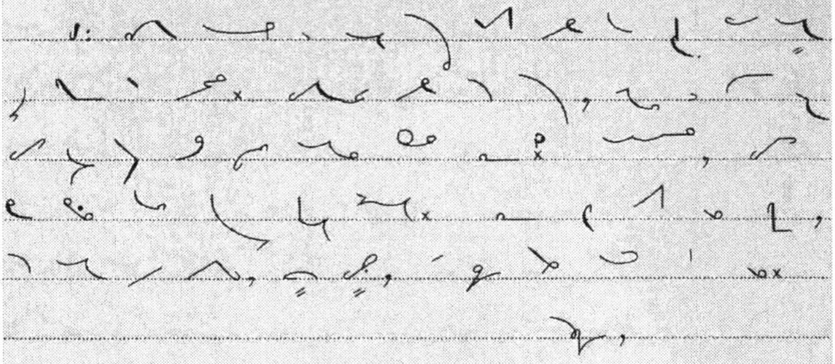

14

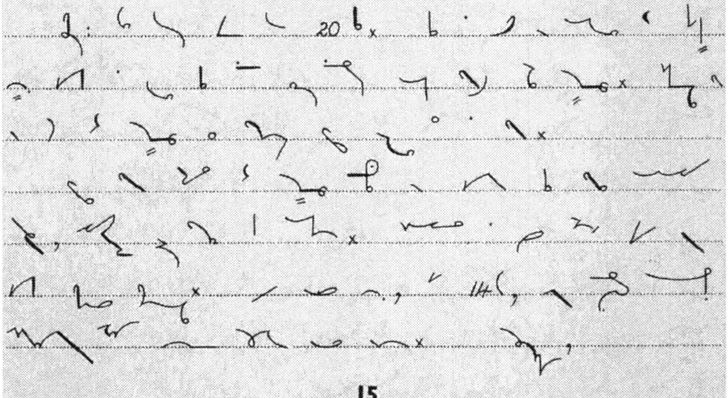

15

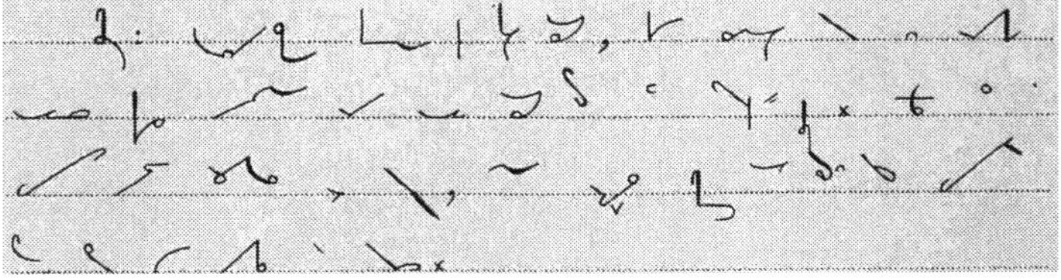

16

17

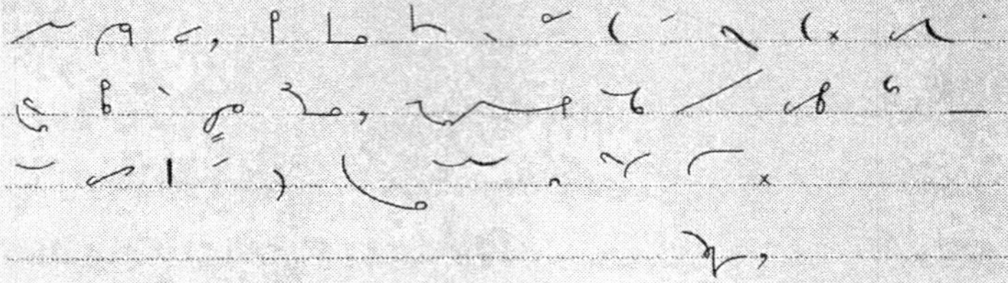

18

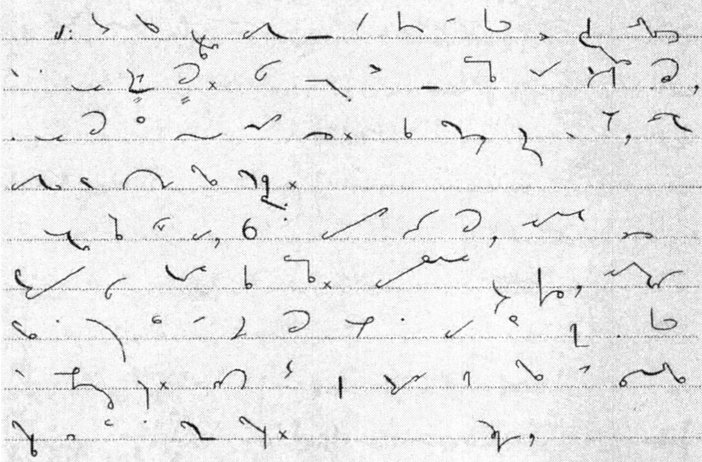

19

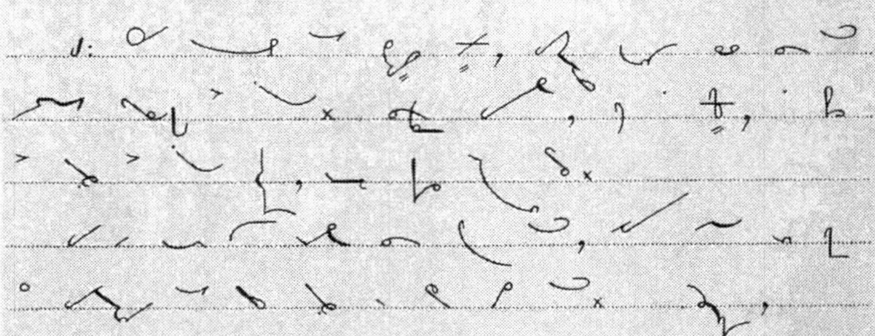

20

21

22

23

24

25

26

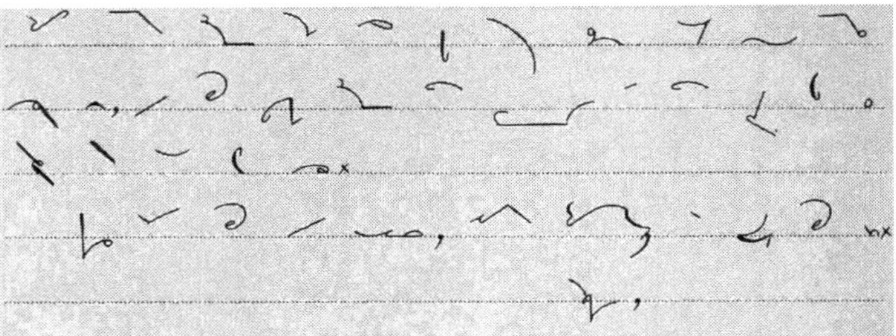

27

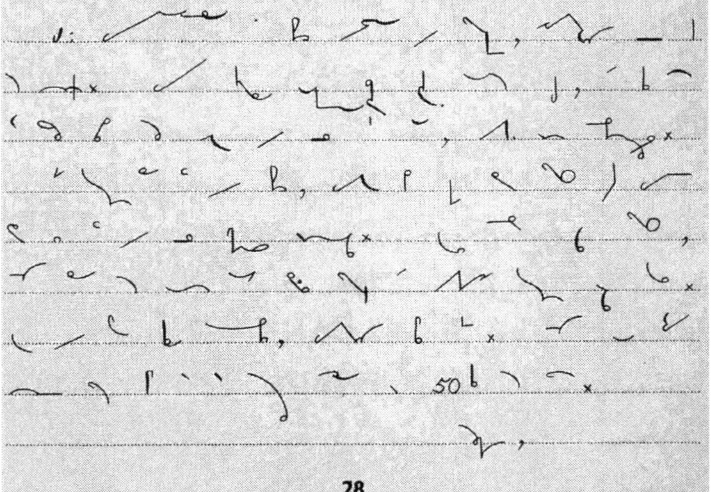

28

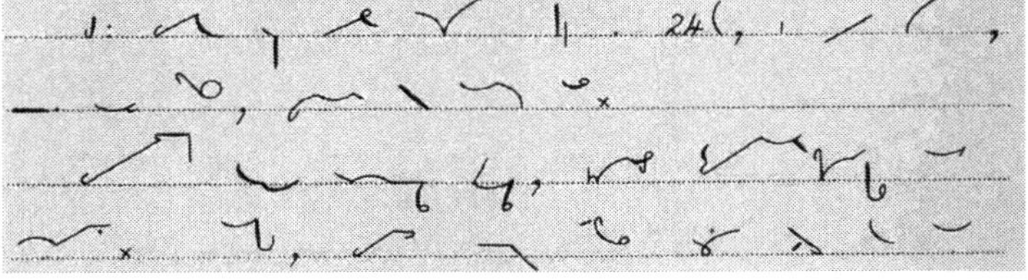

f.o.b.

29

30

31

32

33

34

35

36

37

38

(shorthand outlines)

39

(shorthand outlines)

40

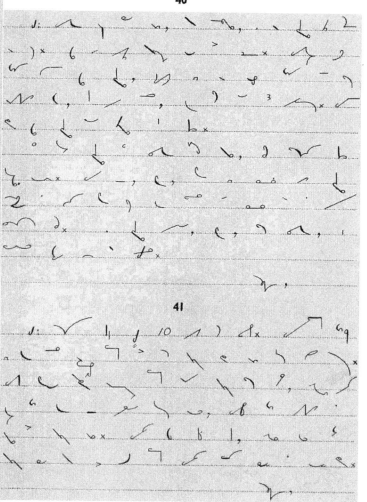

41

42

43

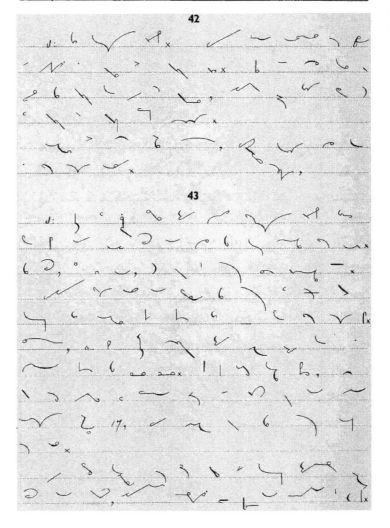

44

45

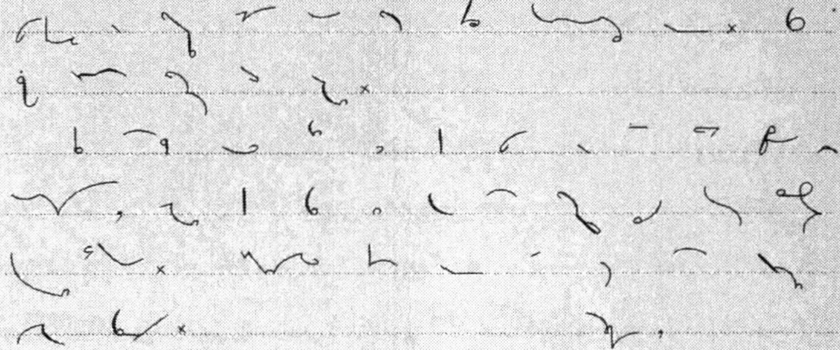

46

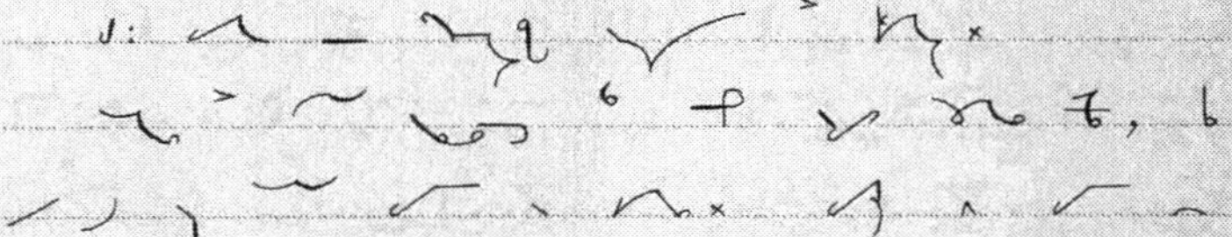

47

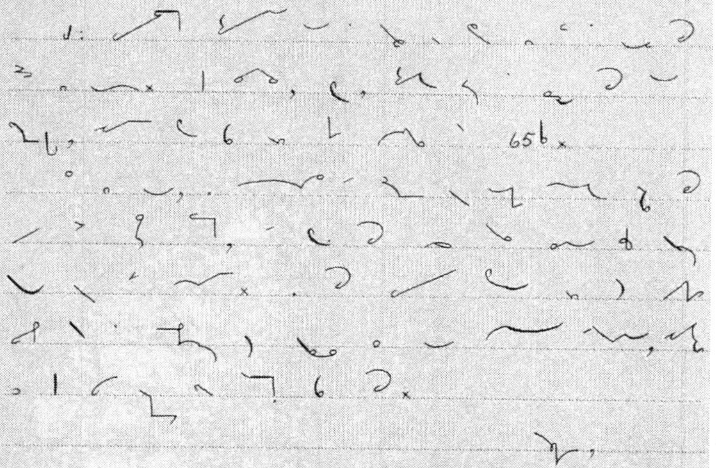

(shorthand notation)

48

(shorthand notation)

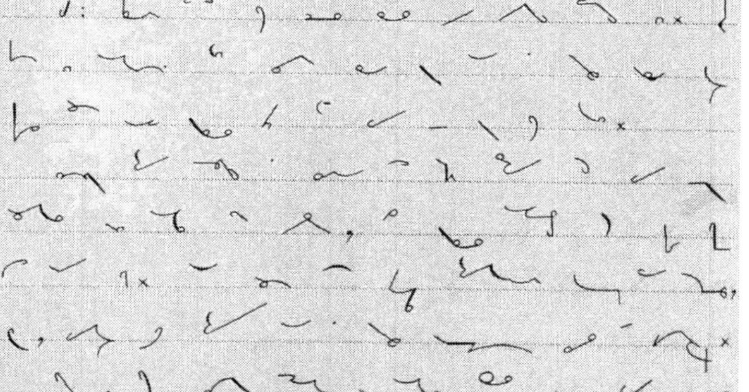

49

50

51

52

53

54

55

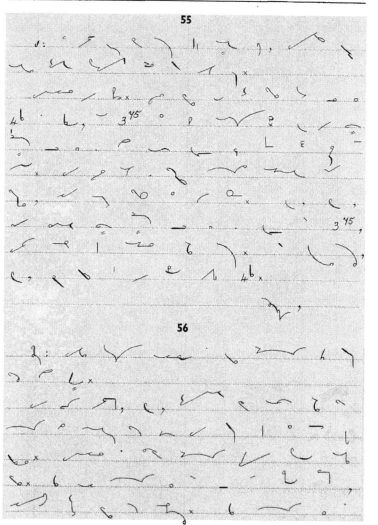

56

57

58

59

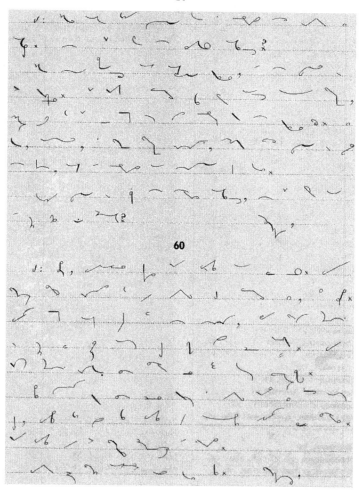

60

INDEX

The figures refer to the page

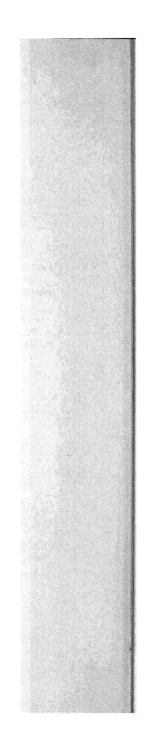